TIME FOR KIDS

Macmillan/McGraw-Hill

Acknowledgments

"I, Too" by Langston Hughes from COLLECTED POEMS Copyright © 1994 by the Estate of Langston Hughes. Reprinted by permission of Alfred Knopf a division of Random House, Inc.

"My Share" by Salih Bolat from THE SAME SKY; A COLLECTION OF POEMS FROM AROUND THE WORLD. An Aladdin Paperback/ An imprint of Simon & Schuster. Reprinted with the permission of Simon and Schuster Children's Publishing Division.

"The Poet Stumbles Upon the Astronomer's Orchards" by Nancy Willard from 19 MASKS FOR THE NAKED POET by Nancy Willard, Copyright © 1984. Reprinted by permission of Houghton Mifflin Harcourt, Inc.

Photography Credits

Book Cover: (c) Jose Luis Pelaez Inc/Blend; (tr) Rana Royalty free/Alamy

Contributor

© Time Inc. All rights reserved. Versions of some articles in this edition of TIME For Kids originally appeared in TIME For Kids or timeforkids.com.

B

 The McGraw·Hill Companies

Macmillan/McGraw-Hill

Published by Macmillan/McGraw-Hill, of McGraw-Hill Education, a division of The McGraw-Hill Companies, Inc., Two Penn Plaza, New York, New York 10121.

Printed in The United States of America

ISBN: 978-0-02-206169-2
MHID: 0-02-206169-X

4 5 6 7 8 9 10 WEB 15 14 13 12 11 10

Contents

Issue 1

Main Idea and Details • Homophones • Time Lines

New Immigrants 6
Coming to America 8
I, Too **POETRY** 12

Issue 2

Main Idea and Details • Idioms • Photos and Captions

Green-Fuel Guide... 14
From Trash to Treasures... 16
Are You Helping? **CHARTS** 20

Issue 3

Main Idea and Details • Inflectional Endings • Time Lines

Honoring Freedom 22
Rebuilding Jamestown 24
Top 10 Historic Sites **TABLES** 28

Issue 4

Problem and Solution • Suffixes • Photos and Captions

Welcome to the City of the Future.............................. 30
All Steamed Up 32
Out of Thin Air **DIAGRAMS** 36

Issue 5

Draw Conclusions • Word Families • Maps

Mount Rushmore Gets a Facial..38
How They Chose These Words for the
   Declaration of Independence...................................40
My Share **POETRY** 44

Issue 6

Sequence • Greek and Latin Roots • Time Lines

Baby Lucy...46
Early Man in America...48
Archaeological Sites in Peru **MAPS** 52

Issue 7

Main Idea and Details • Context Clues
• Skimming and Scanning

The Trail of Tears...54
America in 1850 56
The Path to Independence **TIME LINES** 60

Issue 8

Author's Purpose • Greek and Latin Roots
• Photos and Captions

Free to Celebrate..62
A Melting Pot...64
A Nation of Many Languages **MAPS** 68

Issue 9

Fact and Opinion • Greek Roots • Charts

Why the West is Burning 70

Who is This El Niño Anyway? 72

A Bird Came Down the Walk **POETRY** 76

Issue 10

Description • Multiple-Meaning Words
• Skimming and Scanning

Equal Rights for All 78

It's Our Constitutional Right! 80

How We Elect a President **DIAGRAMS** 84

Issue 11

Fact and Opinion • Antonyms and Synonyms • Diagrams

Catch a Comet by its Tail 86

Look! Up in the Sky! 88

The Poet Stumbles Upon the Astronomer's
Orchards **POETRY** 92

Issue 12

Sequence • Homophones • Tables

Virtual Millions 94

Money Counts 96

Average Allowance **TABLES** 100

Issue 13

Compare and Contrast • Homographs • Tables

Magnetic Earth 102
Richard Serra: Artist 104
Honoring Art and Artists **TABLES** 108

Issue 14

Compare and Contrast • Similes and Metaphors • Maps

Are We Killing the Oceans? 110
Our Packed Planet 112
The Tyger **POETRY** 116

Issue 15

Author's Perspective • Context Clues • Photos and Captions

The Amazing Watson 118
Unraveling a Secret Code 120
Harriet Tubman's Key Dates **TIME LINES** 124

TIME FOR KIDS

Protests by Immigrants

We Are America

America's Newcomers

What challenges do immigrants in the United States face?

New Immigrants

A crowd of immigrants wave flags from the United States and display signs.

Haraz N. Ghanbari/Wide World Photo/AP Images

Thousands of immigrants skip work and school to protest new laws.

One Monday in May 2006, hundreds of thousands of immigrants skipped their daily activities. Workers did not go to their jobs. Students did not go to school. Instead, they spent the day peacefully protesting in cities across the country.

It was called the "Day Without Immigrants." The goal was to show the importance of immigrants to the U.S. economy. There was more to it than staying away from work and school. Many immigrants refused to spend money at stores on that day.

Marchers also called on the government to grant citizenship to illegal immigrants living in the United States.

Thousands of immigrants and supporters took part in the activities. They marched in Los Angeles, Chicago, Houston, Denver, Phoenix, Miami, New York, and other cities.

Giant Work Force

About 800,000 illegal immigrants enter the United States each year. Some sneak across the border. Others get permission for a temporary visit and then stay longer. About 7.2 million illegal immigrants hold jobs in the United States. This estimate comes from the Pew Hispanic Center in Washington, D.C. That is nearly 5 percent of all U.S. workers. Illegal immigrants make up 24 percent of farm workers. They hold 14 percent of construction jobs.

There is now a nationwide debate about illegal immigrants. Some people are in favor of harsh new laws. These laws would send illegal immigrants home and punish those who helped them. Other people are against laws like that. They want a kind solution. They would give those who have been in this country for several years a chance to become legal citizens.

A Fence for the Border

Part of the debate is over a new 700-mile fence. The fence is being built along the border between Mexico and the United States. It is part of a law passed by Congress in 2006. The law aims to stop people in Mexico from illegally entering the United States. President George W. Bush said, "The United States must secure its borders." Vicente Fox, Mexico's president at the time, called the fence "shameful." Critics argue that the fence will not stop illegal immigration. Most illegal immigrants do not enter the country by foot. Instead, they enter by airplane, landing in places like New York or Miami.

Land of Immigrants

No matter what laws are passed, the United States will continue to be a country of immigrants. Out of 300 million Americans in 2006, 34.3 million were born in another country. Experts predict that this number will keep climbing. The importance of immigrants to the country was shown by the 2006 protests. Many farms, factories, markets, and restaurants where illegal immigrants work were closed that day. Melanie Lugo, who marched with her husband and their daughter in Denver, Colorado, said, "We are the backbone of what America is. Legal or illegal, it doesn't matter."

Left Out

In the 1800s Chinese immigrants came to the United States to build a better life. Some Americans blamed low wages and unemployment on the new Chinese workers. Discrimination against Chinese people led to harsh immigration laws.

1825

1849 Large numbers of Chinese come to California for the Gold Rush

1850

1865 Chinese immigrants are recruited to work on the transcontinental railroad

1869 The transcontinental railroad is completed

1875

1880 Over 123,000 Chinese immigrants have entered the United States since 1871

1882 The Chinese Exclusion Act becomes law. It states that no new Chinese workers could come to the United States for the next ten years

1900

1892 The Geary Act renewed the law for ten more years

1902 The Chinese Exclusion Act became permanent

1925

1943 The Chinese Exclusion Act was repealed by the Magnuson Act

1950

COMING TO AMERICA

The nation's newest immigrants share a time-honored dream.

By Joe McGowan

Bettmann/Corbis

▲ Immigrants arrive at Ellis Island in 1920.

The United States is a nation built by immigrants. In the 1840s the first wave came from Ireland, England, and Germany. They found work digging waterways and laying railroad tracks. From 1890 to 1924, a second wave crashed over Ellis Island. Ellis Island is the historic immigration station in New York Harbor. These newcomers left countries such as Italy and Russia. They worked in factories and helped build mighty cities.

Now a new wave of immigrants is coming to America. By the most recent count, some 31 million immigrants live in the United States. They make up 11.5 percent of the population.

Like those who came before, these immigrants arrived hoping to build their own version of the American Dream.

A New Era with New Challenges

Since the September 11, 2001, terrorist attacks, the United States has been rethinking its immigration policy. Some people want to limit the number of new immigrants to 300,000 a year. New rules were made to keep out people who might be terrorists. Because of this, all foreign visitors find it harder to enter the country. Now they face high-tech screening and longer waiting periods. Still, some 3.3 million new immigrants have arrived since January 2000.

Proud, brand-new American citizens
pledge allegiance. ▲

Once here, immigrants need help. "Family is always the first resource," says Lily Woo. She is the principal of Public School 130 in Manhattan, where many Chinese newcomers attend school. Extended immigrant families help one another find housing and work. However, other support groups, like churches and community centers, are not as strong as they once were. As a result, nearly 25 percent of today's immigrant households receive government help. This is usually for health care and school for their children. Some 30 percent of immigrants have not graduated from high school. Many have low-paying jobs.

Melting Pot Is Not As Hot

The United States was sometimes called the great melting pot. People would arrive from all over the world with different cultures, foods, and languages. All the differences "melted" together and formed a single American culture. Without telephones or air travel, those immigrants had to break their ties with their old country.

"Italian immigrants would claim Thomas Jefferson as an ancestor," says Steven Camarota of the Center for Immigration Studies. However, nowadays, says Camarota, those differences disappear more slowly. They don't feel as much pressure to let go of their customs.

RAY KANER

She came to the United States in 1946. Born in Lodz, Poland, she and her husband survived Nazi Germany's concentration camps. Millions of Jewish people died in those camps during World War II.

"I came to New York City after the war. I was 18. Soon after our arrival, my husband became sick and needed to go to a special hospital. Life was difficult, and I was very poor. But I was eager to study and learn. New York State paid for me to take a course at Drake College. For a year I studied typing and other business skills. I knew an immigrant who had been a school principal in Poland. He was a dishwasher in New York.

"I became an American citizen in 1953. This is a wonderful country. As bad as our problems can sound, we still have more freedom than any other place."

◄ Ray Kaner soon after settling on New York City's Lower East Side

America's Newcomers

1607

WHO: Britons
WHY: The British also want the New World's riches. They build their first permanent settlement in Jamestown, Virginia.

1750

WHO: Welsh, Germans, French, Swedes and Finns
WHY: These immigrants want religious freedom. They settle in Pennsylvania, the Carolinas and Delaware.

1500 — **1600** — **1700**

1565

WHO: Spaniards
WHY: Explorers seek the New World's treasures and build the first permanent European settlement in St. Augustine, Florida.

1600s

WHO: Africans
WHY: They are kidnapped and forced to work in the British colonies. The slave trade continues until 1808.

"I'm the luckiest kid in the world," says Prudence Simon, 10, who now lives in New York. "I have two homes, Trinidad and the U.S.A." She is proud to be an American. At the same time, she shows that she is equally proud of her home country.

Some native-born Americans worry that the new immigrants are not eager enough to fit in, or assimilate. Others think that you can be a good American and still hold on to some of the customs and culture of your old country. Only the future will show how the new immigrants will build their American Dream. But one thing is certain: They have a rich history to build on.

Ted Thai

GUO HONG WU

He came to the United States in 2002. Born in southern China, he now lives in New York City with his parents and sister. He has three brothers, who still live in China.

"When I first arrived in New York, I felt scared. I did not trust people. I was worried they would steal money from me.

"In China my mother did not have enough money to buy food. My father is working now and has better job opportunities.

"In New York I get to study more things—animals, nature, American history, and geography. At my school I can read, write, draw, and make books. I hope that one day I can become a scientist."

Guo Hong Wu near an all-American mural at Public School 130 in Manhattan ▶

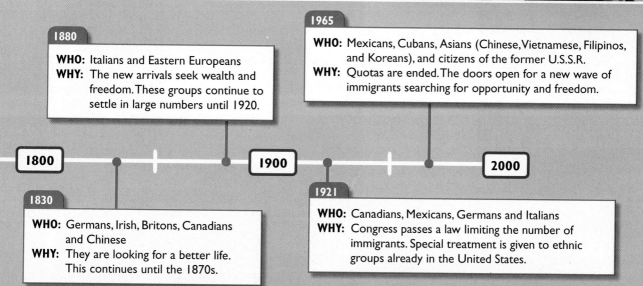

1880
WHO: Italians and Eastern Europeans
WHY: The new arrivals seek wealth and freedom. These groups continue to settle in large numbers until 1920.

1965
WHO: Mexicans, Cubans, Asians (Chinese, Vietnamese, Filipinos, and Koreans), and citizens of the former U.S.S.R.
WHY: Quotas are ended. The doors open for a new wave of immigrants searching for opportunity and freedom.

1800 — **1900** — **2000**

1830
WHO: Germans, Irish, Britons, Canadians and Chinese
WHY: They are looking for a better life. This continues until the 1870s.

1921
WHO: Canadians, Mexicans, Germans and Italians
WHY: Congress passes a law limiting the number of immigrants. Special treatment is given to ethnic groups already in the United States.

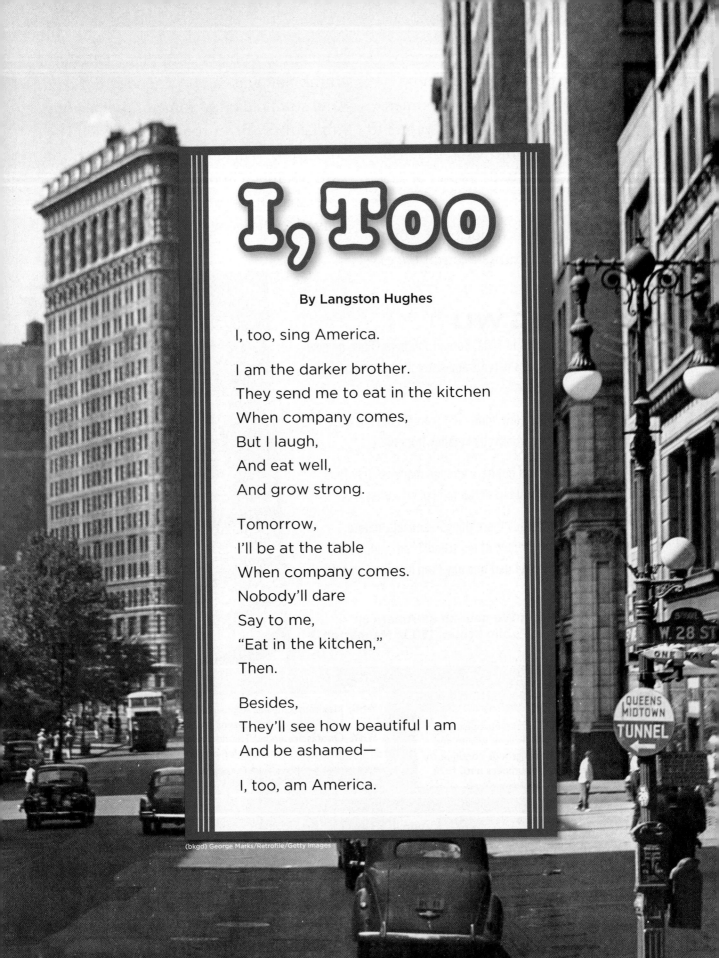

I, Too

By Langston Hughes

I, too, sing America.

I am the darker brother.
They send me to eat in the kitchen
When company comes,
But I laugh,
And eat well,
And grow strong.

Tomorrow,
I'll be at the table
When company comes.
Nobody'll dare
Say to me,
"Eat in the kitchen,"
Then.

Besides,
They'll see how beautiful I am
And be ashamed—

I, too, am America.

TIME
FOR KIDS

Fuel For Thought

THE ART OF RECYCLING

These treasures made from trash are anything but junky.

Green-Fuel Guide

There are plenty of alternatives to gasoline for powering our cars, but choosing one is no piece of cake. — *Susan Moger*

Batteries

What They Are
Storage units for chemical energy that can be converted to electrical energy

Where They Come From
Made from chemicals and other materials

Thumbs Up
Battery-gas hybrids get better mileage per gallon than all-gasoline cars. Batteries are rechargeable and can be recycled. They have the potential to provide cars with a clean source of energy.

Thumbs Down
Hybrids use gasoline, a nonrenewable fossil fuel. Batteries are still not strong enough to power an all-electric car.

Courtesy General Motors Corporation

John B. Carnett

Natural Gas

What It Is
A fossil fuel

Where It Comes From
Extracted from underground

Thumbs Up
Natural gas produces up to 30% less carbon dioxide (a greenhouse gas) than petroleum does. It is produced in the United States.

Thumbs Down
There are few places to fill up a car fueled by natural gas. Pumping natural gas at home is not yet practical. Natural gas is a nonrenewable fuel.

Ethanol

Scott Olson/Getty Images

What It Is
A type of alcohol

Where It Comes From
Most is produced from corn. Some types can be made from sugarcane and other crops.

Thumbs Up
Ethanol is a renewable fuel. The main ingredients come from the United States. Ethanol made from corn can cut greenhouse-gas emissions.

Thumbs Down
Ethanol gets worse mileage than gasoline. It takes a lot of energy to produce and it's not widely available.

Hydrogen

Jim West/Alamy

What It Is
Hydrogen gas (H_2)

Where It Comes From
Doesn't typically exist by itself; produced from compounds; also found in biomass (all plants and animals).

Thumbs Up
Hydrogen-powered cars have zero emissions.

Thumbs Down
Production of hydrogen fuel is expensive and requires electricity which may come from fossil fuels.

Biodiesel

Car Culture/Corbis

What It Is
A combination of plant and animal fat and diesel

Where It Comes From
Ingredients come from vegetable oils, recycled cooking oil, and oil.

Thumbs Up
Biodiesel reduces greenhouse-gas emissions. It gets better mileage per gallon than gasoline. Some of its ingredients are renewable.

Thumbs Down
There is a limited supply of biodiesel fuel, and there are very few places to buy it. Diesel is a nonrenewable fossil fuel.

Diesel

Richard B. Levine/Newscom

What It Is
A fossil fuel

Where It Comes From
Made from oil

Thumbs Up
Diesel-fueled cars get better mileage than gasoline-powered ones. They emit about one-third less carbon dioxide. Diesel fuel is widely available now.

Thumbs Down
Diesel is a nonrenewable fossil fuel and contributes to greenhouse gases.

From Trash to Treasures

An exhibition celebrates creative recycling.

What do you do with your trash? Throw it out? You don't know what you're missing! Look closely at the two figures below. They were made from stuff most people throw away. The figures were crafted from discarded bottle caps.

Those two bottle-cap figures were featured in a museum exhibit called "Recycled, Re-Seen: Folk Art from the Global Scrap Heap." The exhibit was created by the Museum of International Folk Art in Santa Fe, New Mexico. Folk art is art made by ordinary people who have not been trained as artists. Their work is often based on traditions in their culture or community. Fine art, on the other hand, is usually made by people who have had training in art. Works of fine art are valued for their beauty and artistic vision. They are supposed to be looked at but not used. Works of folk art, however, are often made for everyday use.

The Santa Fe show contained more than 800 pieces of folk art from nearly 50 countries. All of the pieces were made from discarded metal, wood, cloth, and plastic. The artists come from many different cultures. Still, they all share one thing. They take objects that are normally thrown away and transform them into objects that are beautiful, useful, and fun. The artists may not think of what they do as recycling, but that's exactly what it is.

John Bigelow Taylor/Shelly Zegart and The Four Corporation/Courtesy Museum of International Folk Art

Capping it off: These two figures are made of bottle caps, wood, and wire.

These dustpans were made in Mexico from old license plates. ▶

Simple Pleasures

Fine artists might work with expensive materials, such as marble, mahogany, and bronze. They might use costly tools to shape these materials into works of art. On the other hand, in poor countries trash might be the only material folk artists and toy makers can afford. The exhibit proves that a rich imagination makes up for poor materials. Seeing toys in castoffs takes a special kind of creativity. A toy film projector from Pakistan, made from cans and machine parts, really works! Shoe-polish cans and bottle caps became a train in India. Some toys offer clues to what life is like for kids in troubled lands. Toys such as tanks and helicopters reflect what people commonly see.

Why are these objects so appealing? They start out as things that are mass-produced by the millions. They end up as one-of-a-kind works of art. All soda cans are alike until someone turns one into an airplane, a truck, or a toy animal. The objects in the exhibit also call attention to recycling. Reducing the amount of trash is an important idea in the modern world.

Artists can take discarded cans and junk and turn them into art. ▼

Recycling Facts

In 2005 the United States created 243 million tons of trash. That's about 4.5 pounds per person per day. Back in 1980 only 15 million tons of trash were recycled in the United States. Compare that with 79 million tons in 2005, thanks to growing awareness and local government rules. Many products today contain recycled material. For example, at least 30 percent of the steel in every can sold in your supermarket is recycled.

The following chart tells the recycling story of some of the most common items found in our trash.

Material	Percent of Total Waste	Percent Recycled	Possible Uses
Paper	34.2	50	Newspapers, comic books, cereal boxes
Plastic	11.9	30	Trash bags, plastic bottles
Glass containers	5.2	25.3	Glass containers
Drink cans	1.4	44.8	Drink cans, anything made of aluminum
Steel	5.9	62	Anything made of steel
Food scraps	11.7	n/a	Compost
Yard trimmings	13.1	61.9	Compost

RECYCLE

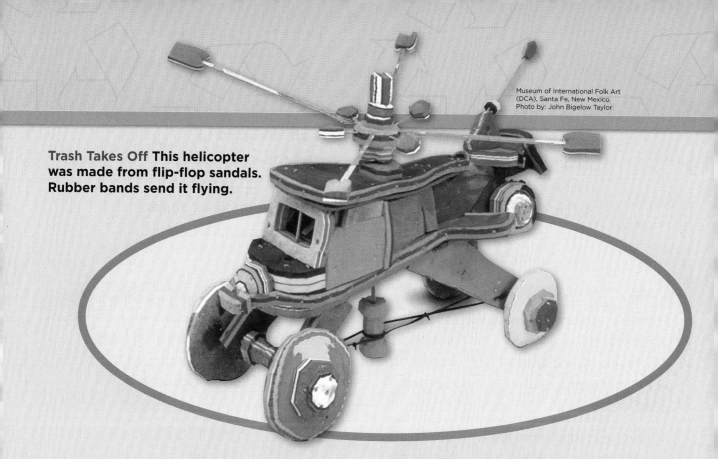

Museum of International Folk Art (DCA), Santa Fe, New Mexico. Photo by: John Bigelow Taylor

Trash Takes Off This helicopter was made from flip-flop sandals. Rubber bands send it flying.

A Long Tradition

Recycled art began long before people began to think about recycling. Some of the objects in the exhibit date from the 1930s. New Mexico has a long tradition of using old tin cans or signs to create new objects. This inspired museum director Charlene Cerny to create the exhibit. Even after finding the pieces, she still had to identify the artists. It wasn't always easy. That's because folk art is often passed down through many hands. There is no trail of sales and owners as there usually is with fine art. Tracking down artists, Cerny says, was like solving "a fantastic mystery."

The exhibition toured the United States, stopping at museums from California to New Jersey. It was a big hit. The show included a workshop where visitors could create their own recycled art. Cerny felt that the show had an important message. It showed creative ways to recycle. But it also reminded kids and adults of the simplicity of playtime. Says Cerny, "You don't have to have a big, expensive toy in order to keep yourself entertained."

So next time you throw out the trash, keep an eye out for treasure.

Are You Helping?

Even if you don't create art out of trash, it's good to conserve our resources. Remember the three Rs: reduce, reuse, recycle. If you reduce waste, reuse things instead of throwing them out, and recycle materials such as paper, plastic, and glass, you will help the environment. Here are tips for conserving our natural resources.

♻ **Reduce**	♻ **Reuse**	♻ **Recycle**
Buy large containers of food. For example, buy a 32-ounce container of yogurt instead of four 8-ounce cups.	Use food containers like egg cartons or coffee cans to store items or to hold paint.	Use cardboard cartons or cereal cartons to collect paper for recycling instead of plastic bags.
When choosing between two similar products, pick the one with the smallest amount of packaging.	Cut old clothes into pieces and use them for rags.	Recycle the cardboard centers of toilet paper.
Tell checkout clerks at stores not to double-wrap items you buy.	Use an eco-friendly reusable tote bag. Reuse paper and plastic bags and tie twists.	Make sure bottles and cans are clean before you put them in the recycling bin.
Turn off the lights and TV when you leave a room.	Write on both sides of paper before throwing it away.	Use products made of recycled materials, including the container.
Fix faucets that drip. One drop per second wastes 540 gallons of water a year.	Fix clothes instead of throwing them away. If possible, repair worn shoes, boots, handbags, and briefcases.	Find out from your community's officials or from a recycling center how materials should be separated for recycling.
	Ship packages in old boxes, using discarded bubble wrap.	If you have a yard, don't remove the grass clippings when the lawn gets mowed. They will decompose and return nutrients to the soil.

WE RECYCLE ♻

TIME
FOR KIDS

Road To Freedom

Digging up the Past

Scientists uncover the secrets of Virginia's colonial Jamestown.

A slave pen like the one recreated at the museum

Honoring Freedom

This museum preserves the story of a historic quest for freedom.

The National Underground Railroad Freedom Center honors those who fought for freedom through the Underground Railroad. The Underground Railroad was a network of people who made it possible for those held in slavery to find freedom. The museum is in Cincinnati, Ohio, just across the Ohio River from Kentucky, a former slave state.

Slavery in the United States

Slavery began in the United States in the 1600s and went on for more than 200 years. In that time millions of people were kidnapped from their homes in Africa and brought to North America as slaves. Even after the slave trade with Africa ended, slavery continued.

The first African slaves came ashore at Jamestown, Virginia, in the 1600s. Over the course of two centuries, slavery took a firm hold in the colonies and remained a part of the new nation. Enslaved people had no rights. Their children were not thought of as their own. Families were torn apart when slaves were sold. Slaves were often abused. They were not permitted an education.

The one bright spot in this terrible history is the story of brave men and women who resisted it. Thousands risked their lives to help enslaved people find freedom. More slaves than we can ever know escaped or resisted their masters.

▲ A slave market

Cruel Reminder—The Slave Pen

One exhibit is called the slave pen. It is the actual wooden structure used by Captain John Anderson, a slave dealer, to lock up his slaves. Visitors can enter the slave pen's cramped space. They can imagine being locked in it with dozens of other enslaved people waiting to be sold.

Slave pens were common sights throughout the upper South, a region important in the interstate slave trade. The exhibit is a chilling reminder of slavery.

Make a Difference

At the Freedom Center, visitors can walk through the Hall of Everyday Heroes and learn about people who helped others find freedom. Naomi Nelson is the center's director of education. She hopes that the museum shows people that they can stand up and make a difference. — *Susan Moger*

◄ **A museum guide talks with kids about slavery.**

▲ **John Rankin's house in Ripley, Ohio**

Next Stop, Freedom!
A time line on the escape from slavery

1738: Fort Moses is founded near St. Augustine, Florida, under Spanish rule. Many slaves from the British colonies escape here. They are given their freedom in exchange for supporting Spain. When Britain takes over Florida in 1763, the ex-slaves go to live in Cuba.

1821: John Rankin publishes *Letters on American Slavery*. An abolitionist, or person who wanted slavery abolished, Rankin goes on to lead hundreds of people to freedom on the Underground Railroad. Rankin was a "conductor," who used his house in Ripley, Ohio, as a "stop," or safe place, for escaped slaves (called "packages").

1831: The organized system started by abolitionists to help runaway slaves is first given the name Underground Railroad.

1850: Harriet Tubman makes the first of her 19 trips to the South to escort escaped slaves to their freedom. Over the next ten years, she personally brings 300 slaves north.

1865: The Thirteenth Amendment to the Constitution abolishes slavery in the United States.

Rebuilding Jamestown

The first permanent English settlement in the United States is rebuilt.

▲ Visitors to Jamestown National Park in Virginia can watch archaeologists search for buried treasure at the colonists' original fort.

Jamestown, Virginia, has come back to life. After years of searching, archaeologists have found the original foundations of the first permanent English settlement in North America. Now, 400 years after it was first built, the wooden walls are rising again in exactly the same place.

The original colonists arrived in 1607 and built a triangle-shaped fort. But by the 1700s, the town no longer existed. Historians had long thought that whatever remained of the fort was lost under the river. Now the fort has been rediscovered—on dry land.

Not Built to Last

On May 13, 1607, a ship carrying 104 men and boys from England arrived at a pear-shaped peninsula in Virginia. The site was named Jamestown after Britain's King James. Using old-fashioned spelling, Captain John Smith described the spot as "a verie fit place for the erecting of a great cittie."

The area was the home of a Native American people called the Powhatan. They were one of the many Algonquian nations that lived on the east coast of North America. The colonists built a fort along the river to protect themselves from the Spanish, who were settling in Florida. They also needed protection from the Powhatan. Only 34 of the colonists survived the first year. Many of the colonists died from disease, starvation, and fighting with the Native Americans. In 1608 a fire destroyed the fort.

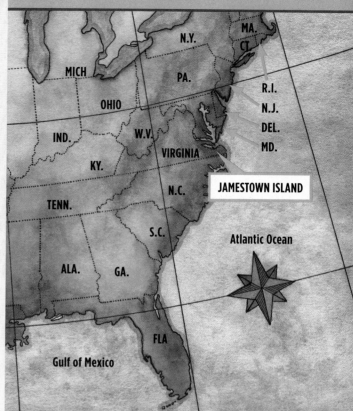

▲ A model shows how the 1607 fort once looked.

Jamestown survived and became the capital of the Virginia colony. In 1698 another fire burned down important buildings there. Eventually, the governor of Virginia moved the capital to nearby Williamsburg. Old Jamestown began to disappear—at least above ground.

Dusting Off History

But what about underground? During the 1940s and 1950s, archaeologists began to explore and dig in parts of Jamestown. They found many artifacts but believed that the original fort must have washed away.

Location of Jamestown

Jamestown was the first permanent English settlement in America. Colonists built it in 1607 on Jamestown Island, off the coast of Virginia. The picture below shows what the town might have looked like before it burnt down.

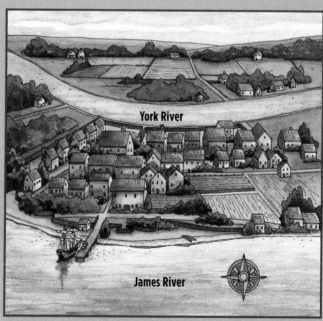

Copper pennies were probably traded between settlers and Native Americans. ▼

▲ A family crest on this brass ring links it to William Strachey, secretary of the colony in 1610.

Archaeologist Bill Kelso didn't think so. In April 1994 he and others began digging at a tempting new spot. "There was a piece of ground, shaped like a triangle, that no one had ever put a shovel into." His hunch paid off. Kelso and his team soon found bits of pottery that could only have been from the 1607 fort. "That first day we knew we had found it!" he exclaimed.

Since then archaeologists have uncovered more than 180,000 artifacts from the early 1600s, including beads, keys, and toys. And only a fraction of the fort's grounds have been explored!

"We don't dig things up, we uncover them," says Kelso. The process requires great care. "You just can't hurry it up."

One corner of the fort is in the river, but most of it is on dry land. In the first season of digging, the team found the south wall, or palisade, of the fort. All that remained were stains in the ground from the rotted wood of the walls along with the holes where the posts had been. In the second year, they found the tower, or bulwark, that stood in one corner of the triangle.

Using a tiny 1608 drawing as a guide, the searchers looked for a second wall. They found it. They also found that the two walls formed an angle, exactly as the historical record described it.

Clues to Colonial Life

The discoveries are giving experts a picture of how early colonists lived and died. "Archaeology is like a time machine," says Kelso.

Pistols, knives, and heavy armor tell the story of a violent time. But, says Kelso, "we started finding copper, copper, copper—just piles of it!" Colonists may have used this precious metal to buy peace with the Powhatan.

▲ **Settlers seem to have tossed garbage, including fish bones and waste iron, into deep pits like this one at the fort site.**

Some of the most intriguing finds are a few skeletons of the first settlers. Anthropologist Doug Owsley of the Smithsonian Institute is thrilled to study these remains. "Bones tell you stories of what life was like for those people, what killed them, even what they ate," Owsley says.

One skeleton was found with a musket ball in its right leg. Scientists think it is the remains of a teenager who may have bled to death from the wound. Who shot him, and why? It's a colonial murder mystery!

Rebuilding the Past

As of 2006 the remains of all three of the fort's walls and several buildings had been uncovered. To help visitors picture the old settlement, researchers have begun to build new wooden walls in the same locations as the old ones. Meanwhile more discoveries remain ahead. Jamestown has been found at last.

Early Colonies

Explorers and settlers came to North America from Europe for many reasons. Some came in search of great riches. Others hoped to find a route to Asia. Many wanted to make a new life. Here are just a few of the places where they settled.

1550

1565 St. Augustine, Florida

The oldest permanent European settlement in America is founded by the Spanish admiral Pedro Menéndes de Avilés. It is a Spanish Colonial city for over 200 years.

1607 Jamestown, Virginia

The first permanent English settlement in America is established. It is named in honor of King James I.

1608 Quebec, Canada

The first permanent French settlement in North America is founded by Samuel de Champlain. From this location the French later explored the Great Lakes and the Mississippi River.

1600

1624 Albany, New York

About 30 Dutch families settled Fort Orange. The settlement was a part of New Netherland which claimed land along the Hudson River. Two years later the Dutch purchased Manhattan Island from the Manahates Indians.

1620 Plymouth, Massachusetts

After a three-month voyage aboard the Mayflower, the Pilgrims arrived in Plymouth. Religious conflicts led the Pilgrims to leave England for the Netherlands and then North America.

1650

Top 10 Historic Sites

There are nearly 400 parks, monuments, and recreation areas in the U.S. National Park Service. Many have great historic importance to Americans. Here are the most popular historic sites in 2005.

Rank	National Park Site	Visitors
1	Great Smoky Mountains National Park	9,192,477
2	National World War II Memorial	4,410,379
3	Grand Canyon National Park	4,401,522
4	Statue of Liberty National Monument	4,235,595
5	San Francisco Maritime National Historical Park	3,976,056
6	Independence National Historical Park	3,951,073
7	Vietnam Memorial	3,799,968
8	Lincoln Memorial	3,638,806
9	Castle Clinton National Memorial	3,487,307
10	Colonial National Historical Park	3,338,695

Scott Smith/Corbis

The National World War II Memorial is in Washington, D.C.

Grand Canyon N.P.

The Grand Canyon National Park is located in Arizona.

The Great Smoky Mountains National Park stretches from Tennessee to North Carolina.

(bkgd) James L. Amos/Corbis

TIME FOR KIDS

Steam Heat!

In some countries geothermal power is becoming a hot source for clean, renewable energy.

Welcome to the City of the future

Clean energy and "green" buildings will change the way we live in the future.

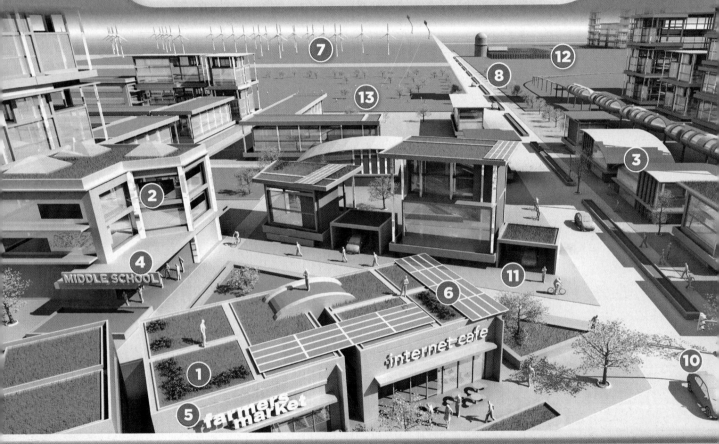

Bryan Christie

Most scientists now say that human activities have played a significant role in global warming.

As a result, scientists, architects, business leaders, and lawmakers are creating programs to encourage more Earth-friendly living. The number of energy-smart communities is on the rise. Here's what a town could look like in the near future if people were to put more energy into taking care of the environment.

The Green House

Energy-saving homes and buildings conserve water and energy. Grass- and plant-covered rooftops (1) absorb less heat and act as filters for rainwater harvesting. Rainwater is collected and stored. It is later used to flush toilets and water plants. Open windows (2) act as air conditioners. Geothermal heat pumps use water to cool the home in summer and keep it warm in winter. Some homes (3) are made from recycled materials. In green schools (4), teachers use hands-on lessons to teach kids about the environment. Stores and offices (5) are within walking distance of homes. Markets sell locally grown food.

Clean Power

Solar panels, wind turbines, hydropower, and geothermal energy use the power of nature to generate electricity and make things run. Solar panels (6) turn the sun's energy into electricity to power homes. Wind turbines (7), arranged in large groups called wind farms, convert the energy of the wind into electricity. Hydropower harnesses energy from flowing water.

Geothermal energy draws heat from deep within Earth's interior. These sources release much less carbon dioxide.

Alternative Transportation

Cars, trucks, and buses run on renewable fuels. Ethanol is made from corn or grasses (8). Biodiesel fuel comes from soybeans and cooking grease. Alternative-power vehicles and mass transit, such as light-rail trains (9), reduce the use of gasoline. Hybrid cars (10) combine fuel-burning engines and battery-powered motors. Electric cars (11) run on batteries that are charged the same way as laptop computer batteries.

Open Spaces

Backyards are used for composting. Food, paper, and yard waste break down quickly to create rich soil for gardening (12). Recycling is as common as taking out the trash. Even land is recycled. Former airports and dumps are cleaned up and turned into parks (13). — *Angelique LeDoux*

All Steamed Up

Natural heat from deep inside Earth is also a clean source of energy here on the surface.

Xianyang, China, is one of the most polluted cities in China. Most of the pollution is caused by coal that's burned to generate much of the city's power. The air in Reykjavík, Iceland, though, is crystal clear. That's because no fuel is burned there. Iceland's capital gets 100% of its heat and 40% of its electricity from renewable energy sources.

Now, engineers from Iceland are working with the Chinese to help clean up the air in Xianyang. If they are successful, the city will have the biggest geothermal system in the world.

Reuters/Stringer Shanghai

Some cities in China are among the most polluted in the world.

Steam rises from geothermal vents.

What Is Geothermal Energy?

Geo means "earth," and *thermal* means "heat." Geothermal power is power that comes from our planet's heat. In Iceland there are 130 volcanoes bringing heat from deep inside Earth to the surface of the land.

It's easiest to tap geothermal energy where hot magma is nearest to the surface. Cold water from the surface seeps into the ground and when it hits hot, molten rock, the result is steam. Steam power is a clean, renewable energy source that can run engines, heat homes, and turn on lights. Geothermal power plants capture steam below the surface, pump it out, and use it to turn turbines. A turbine is a big shaft with blades attached, like a fan. The turning blades generate electricity.

Geothermal power can provide clean, renewable energy to cities and towns.

Peter Parks/Getty Images

Steam Heat in China

If the team of Chinese and Icelandic engineers is successful, Xianyang will become a model for future use of geothermal power. Meanwhile, there are plans in place to tap geothermal energy in other parts of the country. Geothermal pumps were part of the heating and cooling systems of some of the venues at the 2008 Olympic Games in Beijing.

There are geothermal resources in almost every province in China, so geothermal energy pumps could be used across the entire country. That would be good for everyone. Last year alone, China added 102 gigawatts to its electrical grid. That's about twice as much energy as is used in all of California. Approximately 90% of that energy came from carbon-belching coal plants. Geothermal energy can at least start to clean up China's air. *— Lisa Jo Rudy*

Geothermal Energy in the United States

The United States produces more geothermal electricity than any other country in the world! Geothermal energy is usually found in areas where there are earthquakes and volcanoes. Consequently, only four states currently have geothermal power plants. They are: California, Hawaii, Nevada, and Utah.

California is a geologically active place. It is located along the Ring of Fire. This is a belt that circles the Pacific Ocean. As a result, it's ideal for producing geothermal energy. In San Bernardino, geothermal energy is used to heat more than 30 buildings. When added together, California's geothermal power plants produce about 40 percent of the world's geothermally generated electricity.

The Geysers is a geothermal power plant north of San Francisco. It first started operating in 1960. At the Geysers, high temperature steam is tapped to turn turbines and generate electricity.

The Geysers

Courtesy Calpine

The Cascade Mountain Range is a source of geothermal energy in North America. It extends from British Columbia, Canada to California and has active volcanoes.

The Best of Nature/Alamy

Out of Thin Air

Using the wind to do work is a very old idea. Ancient people figured out that wind pushing against a sail could move a ship. Later, people learned how to use windmills to move machinery that could grind corn and wheat, saw wood, and pump water. In the 1920s, Americans were using windmills to generate electricity on a small scale.

Today, we have the technology to use wind to generate electricity on a larger scale. It's done on wind farms, where dozens of large machines called turbines harness the power of the wind. Here's how it works.

Wind Turbine

▼ Wind makes the blades turn.

◀ The turning blades cause the shaft to spin.

◀ The spinning shaft is connected to a generator. The generator changes the mechanical energy released by the spinning into electrical energy.

◀ The electricity is carried through cables to homes, businesses, and schools.

Energy Riddle

Why is wind energy really solar energy?

Answer: Wind is moving air. Heat from the Sun makes air move. So wind energy really comes from the Sun.

Rob Schuster

TIME FOR KIDS

MOUNTAIN MEN

The famous faces of Mount Rushmore are getting a facial.

Mount Rushmore
Gets a Facial

▲ **Workers prepare Thomas Jefferson's face for power washing.**

Doug Dreyer/AP Images

The most famous men carved in rock are getting free facials.

For 65 years the granite faces of Mount Rushmore have looked out into rain, snow, heat, and wind. In all that time, they were never washed—until recently. In 2005, using a chemical-free pressurized water system heated to more than 200 degrees, workers scrubbed the faces clean.

The Mount Rushmore National Monument consists of the giant heads of Presidents George Washington, Thomas Jefferson, Abraham Lincoln, and Theodore Roosevelt. The faces are carved in the granite mountain, about 35 miles south of Rapid City, South Dakota. The monument attracts almost three million visitors each year.

Cleaning the Peaks

Geologists say that granite, which can stand up to all sorts of weather, can erode approximately one inch every 10,000 years. However, since its completion in 1941, the monument has gathered decades of dirt and grime. Growing on the dirt are lichen, organisms that are a combination of fungus and algae.

North Dakota

South

Mount
Rushmore

☆ Pierre

Dakota

Nebraska

Colorado

Burgandy Beam

Lichen can create cracks and crevices. In winter the cracks get wider from water freezing and expanding in the cracks. If allowed to continue, this wears away and damages the stone more quickly.

A Massive Cleaning Job

The cleanup was done by a German company, which offered to do the job for free. According to Thorsten Mowes, the head of the cleaning project, the hardest part was getting to the monument. The crews could not build a scaffold, so they had to walk up to the top. Cables with saddles at the end were anchored to the top. Cleaning crews then lowered themselves onto the front of each head for a power wash.

When the crews arrived, the giant sculptures, though in need of cleaning, were still awe inspiring. "I was very proud to be eye to eye with George Washington," said Mowes.

The purpose of the cleaning was not only to get rid of grime but also to preserve the carvings. "The average visitor [won't] be able to tell the difference," said Duane Bubac, Mount Rushmore facilities manager.

Although the work was difficult, the cleaning crews did have one lucky break. Since the sculptures are just faces, the workers didn't have to wash behind the Presidents' ears.

The Faces of Mount Rushmore: George Washington, Thomas Jefferson, Theodore Roosevelt, and Abraham Lincoln ▼

JP Laffont/Sygma/Corbis

HOW THEY CHOSE THESE WORDS FOR THE
Declaration of Independence

The writing of the Declaration of Independence was assigned to Thomas Jefferson, but he had some help.

In 1776 the Continental Congress prepared to vote on the question of American independence. But before it could vote, Congress needed a written declaration to explain the decision.

Congress established a distinguished committee to draft the Declaration of Independence.

It included Benjamin Franklin, John Adams, Connecticut merchant Roger Sherman, and New York lawyer Robert Livingston. Thomas Jefferson was the chairman of the committee. It was his job to write the first draft of the declaration.

Jefferson was only 33 and was not the most important person on the committee. So why was he the writer? Other members of the committee were involved in other work that they felt was more important. Benjamin Franklin was sick in bed.

So Jefferson sat down to write the Declaration of Independence. He wrote in a home on Market Street in Philadelphia. He started with the words "When in the course of human events . . ."

His writing went on to attack the King of England. In those days, attacking the King in writing meant you were declaring a revolution.

Jefferson used his own poetic style of writing. He drew a lot of his ideas and words, though, from other writers. He sounded a bit like Benjamin Franklin. He sounded a little like the philosopher John Locke. He actually copied from the Declaration of Rights that George Mason had written for the Constitution of Virginia. In those days, copying was considered to be proper and showed that you had read a great deal.

Thomas Jefferson ▼

Once he finished his draft, Jefferson showed it to Franklin. Franklin made some changes. Among other things, he changed the phrase "We hold these truths to be sacred and undeniable" to the now-famous words "We hold these truths to be self-evident."

On July 2, 1776, the Continental Congress read Jefferson's Declaration. They made a great many changes, and Jefferson was quite upset. Finally, though, the entire Congress agreed on a single document.

At the official signing of the parchment copy on August 2, John Hancock, the president of the Congress, penned his name with his famous flourish. "There must be no pulling different ways," he declared. "We must all hang together." According to the early American historian Jared Sparks, Franklin replied, "Yes, we must, indeed, all hang together, or most assuredly we shall all hang separately." — *Lisa Jo Rudy*

▲ **Benjamin Franklin, John Adams, and Thomas Jefferson working on the Declaration of Independence**

The signed Declaration of Independence ▶

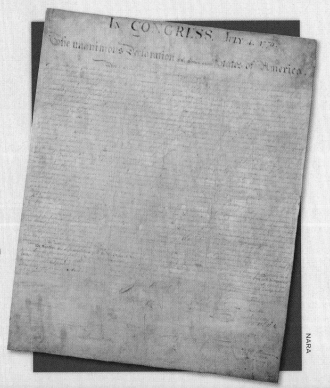

Philadelphia, Pennsylvania

Did you know Philadelphia was our nation's capital from 1790 to 1800? Today it is home to many historic landmarks. Independence Hall, where the Declaration of Independence was signed, is located in Philadelphia. The Liberty Bell is too. Other sights include the Betsy Ross House, the First Bank of the United States, and Elfreth's Alley, one of our nation's oldest residential streets. This map will help you explore the extraordinary sites of historic Philadelphia.

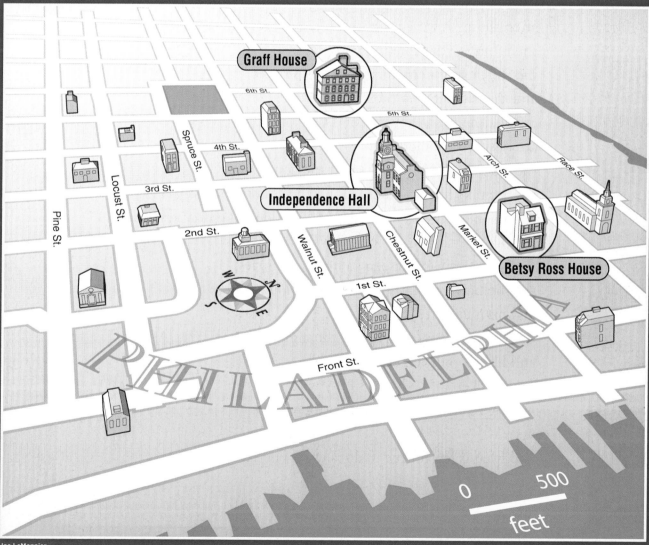

Joe LeMonnier

My Share

By Salih Bolat
(Translated by Yusuf Eradam)

everyone's busy with something
that granny spinning wool
with hands like dried, shrunken cucumbers
left in the field
after the seeds were taken out,
she is busy with something;
the wheeler-dealer who buys and sells land
and the student who is examined
on what he wasn't taught
are busy with something;
the cashier who wonders about the connection
between his hands and the money he counts endlessly
and the manager who married off his elder daughter yesterday,
the pilot getting ready for a new flight
with his bag that has seen so many countries,
the fireman who has spent a day without trouble
and his memories of fires,
the worker who wakes up for the night shift
and his sleeping anger,
that chicken in the litter is busy with something
getting ready for chicks like cotton-candy,

and what is left for me to do is write poetry.

TIME

FOR KIDS

Oldest Baby?

First Americans

A 9,400-year-old skeleton reveals new clues about our earliest history.

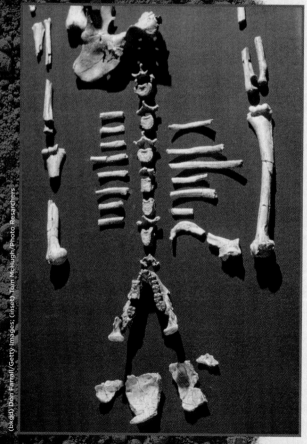

A scientist holds the skull of Selam.

Baby Lucy

The fossil of an ancient child is found in Ethiopia.

Scientists hunting for fossils in Ethiopia made a major discovery. Along the Great Rift Valley, they found the fossil skeleton of a child. It is the oldest and most complete skeleton of an ancient human ever found.

The bones are the remains of a three-year-old who lived 3.3 million years ago. Her species is called *Australopithecus afarensisa*. The scientists have named the skeleton Selam, which means "peace" in the Amharic language of Ethiopia.

Selam's discovery was especially exciting to scientists. That's because it is the same species as another fossil, nicknamed Lucy. Selam, also known as Baby Lucy, was found very close to the area where Lucy was uncovered. When Lucy was discovered in 1974, it was the oldest known human fossil. Selam is about 150,000 years older.

◀ **This is the skeleton of Lucy. She was about four feet tall.**

Euan Denholm/Reuters/Newscom

(bkgd) Don Farrall/Getty Images; (inset) Tom McHugh/Photo Researchers

Found in the Desert

Selam was discovered by a team of fossil hunters led by Dr. Zeresenay Alemseged. Alemseged is an Ethiopian scientist who started his research in northeastern Ethiopia in 1999. The big discovery came in 2000. First, one of the team saw the face of the skeleton in a block of sandstone. It was clear to the researchers that they were looking at the face of a young afarensis.

Then, the scientists began the process of getting the skeleton out of the sandstone. They had to be very careful not to damage the bones. The team used small dentists' drills and picks. When they uncovered the skeleton's hands, the one complete finger was curled in a tiny grasp. Finally, after five years of work, most of the fossil parts had been removed.

Selam is now in a laboratory in Addis Ababa, Ethiopia's capital. Alemseged and other scientists continue to study the fossil bones. This discovery shows that there are still important fossils waiting to be found. Scientists in Ethiopia, in other parts of Africa, and all around the world continue searching for clues to how humans lived thousands of years ago. Human history is still being uncovered, one bone at a time.

Selam was discovered in the Dikika region of Ethiopia. She was found close to where Lucy was uncovered.

AFRICA

ERITREA
SUDAN
DJIBOUTI
SOMALIA
Addis Ababa
DIKIKA
ETHIOPIA
KENYA

N W E S

KEY
★ = Capital

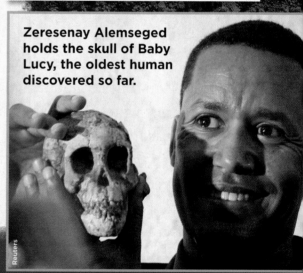

Zeresenay Alemseged holds the skull of Baby Lucy, the oldest human discovered so far.

Reuters

Fossil Finds

Many important discoveries about human history have been made in East Africa.

1950   1970   1990   2010

1959: Mary Leakey discovers Nutcracker Man at Olduvai Gorge, Tanzania

1974: Donald Johanson discovers Lucy at Hadar, Ethiopia

1978: Footprints discovered at Laetoli, Tanzania

2000: Dr. Zeresenay Alemseged discovers Selam at Dikika, Ethiopia

Early Man in America

An ancient skeleton helps us understand our continent's past.

By Michael D. Lemonick and Andrea Dorfman

Two college students found the skull on a bank of the Columbia River near Kennewick, Washington, in the summer of 1996. Later, more bones were recovered. They looked old, but scientists were surprised to learn just how old they really were. Tests showed that the skeleton, which came to be known as Kennewick Man, is 9,400 years old. It is among the oldest and most complete skeletons ever found in the Americas. Only about 50 skeletons that old have ever been found on either continent.

Scientists were eager to study Kennewick Man. But for about nine years, the bones were caught in a tug-of-war among Native American groups, the U.S. government, which owns the land where the bones were found, and scientists. The Native American groups wanted the skeleton treated with respect and reburied. They claimed the bones under the Native American Graves Protection and Repatriation Act. A group of researchers sued for the right to examine the bones. Finally in 2005, scientists got to study Kennewick Man for just ten days.

Chip Clark/Smithsonian

▲ Douglas Owsley examines the pieces of Kennewick Man's skull.

What the Bones Reveal

Douglas Owsley works at the Smithsonian Institution's National Museum of Natural History in Washington, D.C. He and the team examined the skeleton and made strong guesses about what Kennewick Man looked like. They suspect that he was about 38 years old when he died. He was about 5 feet 9 inches tall, fairly muscular, and right-handed. He had suffered several injuries, including a spear jab to his hip. "The injury looks healed," Owsley told TIME.

A Story Told by Bones

Scientists have up to 90 percent of Kennewick Man's skeleton. They are testing the bones to see if they can figure out what he ate, how he was killed, and other facts about his life.

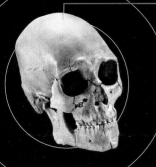

Family Tree Researchers made this copy of the skull. Its features suggest that Kennewick Man may have had an Asian background.

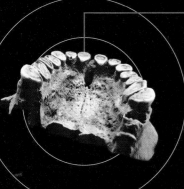

Big Smile Wear patterns on the surfaces of the teeth suggest that whatever Kennewick Man ate, a lot of sand and grit came with it. Yuck!

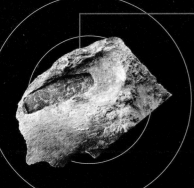

Battle Wounds A stone spear tip is stuck in the hip. This attack did not kill the man.

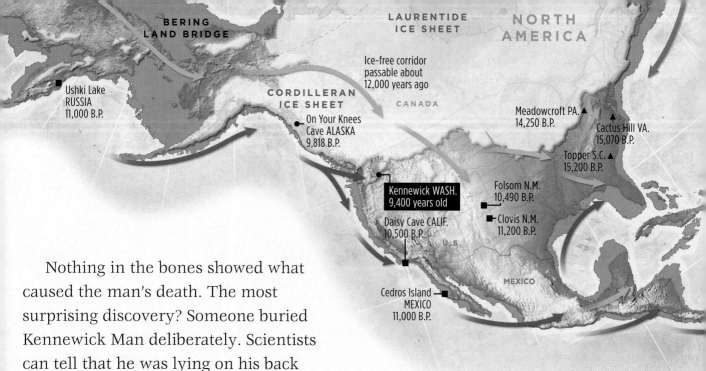

BERING
LAND BRIDGE

LAURENTIDE
ICE SHEET

NORTH
AMERICA

Ice-free corridor
passable about
12,000 years ago

CORDILLERAN
ICE SHEET

CANADA

Ushki Lake
RUSSIA
11,000 B.P.

On Your Knees
Cave ALASKA
9,818 B.P.

Meadowcroft PA.
14,250 B.P.

Cactus Hill VA.
15,070 B.P.

Topper S.C.
15,200 B.P.

Kennewick WASH.
9,400 years old

Folsom N.M.
10,490 B.P.

Daisy Cave CALIF.
10,500 B.P.

Clovis N.M.
11,200 B.P.

U.S.

MEXICO

Cedros Island
MEXICO
11,000 B.P.

Nothing in the bones showed what caused the man's death. The most surprising discovery? Someone buried Kennewick Man deliberately. Scientists can tell that he was lying on his back with his feet rolled slightly outward and his arms at his sides.

Still, the bones have many more secrets to reveal. Researchers say further tests may show what killed Kennewick Man and even what he ate. "We can tell if he ate nothing but plants, predominantly meat, or a mixture of the two," says team member Thomas Stafford.

Who Discovered America?

Kennewick Man may help scientists solve mysteries about where the earliest Americans came from and when they got here. Archaeologists (ahr•kee•OL•uh•jists) are scientists who study ancient people and artifacts. For decades they believed that the earliest Americans arrived from Asia about 12,000 years ago. According to this theory, ancient people walked across dry land that once connected what is now Russia with Alaska. From there, the theory goes, they made their way south.

But discoveries since the 1980s are pushing that idea aside. Recent finds at Monte Verde, Chile, and Daisy Cave, California, suggest that bands of people moved down the Pacific coast of North and South America much earlier than 12,000 years ago.

Artifacts discovered in South Carolina have led a few archaeologists to say that early Americans might even have arrived on the Atlantic coast from Europe.

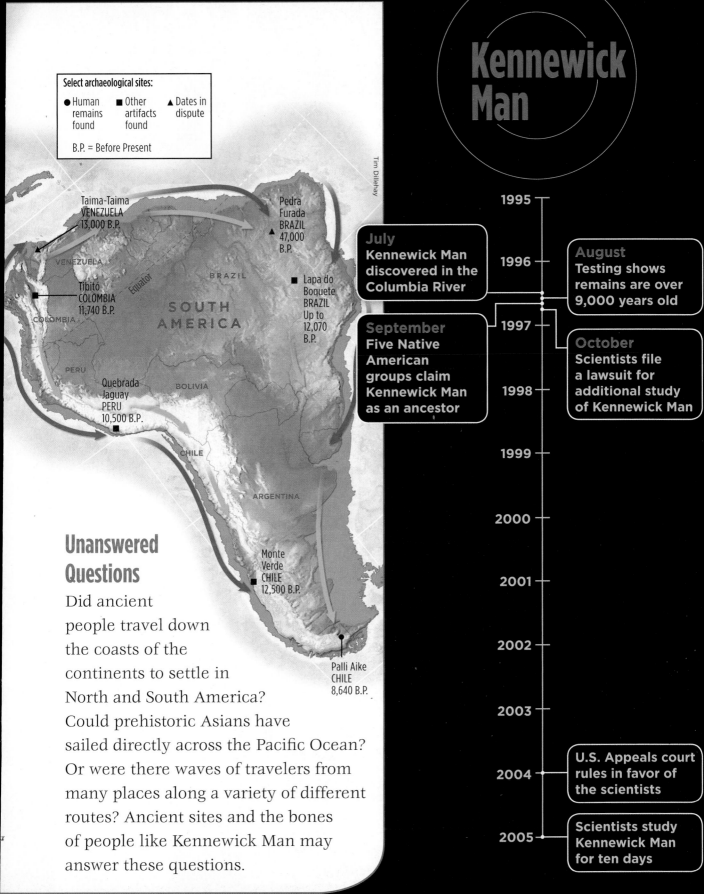

Kennewick Man

Select archaeological sites:

● Human remains found
■ Other artifacts found
▲ Dates in dispute

B.P. = Before Present

Tim Dillehay

SOUTH AMERICA

Equator

Taima-Taima
VENEZUELA
13,000 B.P.

VENEZUELA

Tibitó
COLOMBIA
11,740 B.P.

COLOMBIA

Pedra Furada
BRAZIL
47,000 B.P.

BRAZIL

Lapa do Boquete
BRAZIL
Up to 12,070 B.P.

PERU

Quebrada Jaguay
PERU
10,500 B.P.

BOLIVIA

CHILE

ARGENTINA

Monte Verde
CHILE
12,500 B.P.

Palli Aike
CHILE
8,640 B.P.

Unanswered Questions

Did ancient people travel down the coasts of the continents to settle in North and South America? Could prehistoric Asians have sailed directly across the Pacific Ocean? Or were there waves of travelers from many places along a variety of different routes? Ancient sites and the bones of people like Kennewick Man may answer these questions.

1995

1996

1997

1998

1999

2000

2001

2002

2003

2004

2005

July
Kennewick Man discovered in the Columbia River

August
Testing shows remains are over 9,000 years old

September
Five Native American groups claim Kennewick Man as an ancestor

October
Scientists file a lawsuit for additional study of Kennewick Man

U.S. Appeals court rules in favor of the scientists

Scientists study Kennewick Man for ten days

Archaeological Sites in Peru

Humans first settled in Peru more than 7,000 years ago. The country has many ruins of ancient cities and tombs filled with treasures. This map shows just some of the fascinating sites that archaeologists have found.

Equator

ECUADOR

COLOMBIA

Amazon River

PERU

BRAZIL

Miles
0   50   100
0   100   200
Kilometers

Lord of Sipán
Ruler buried with hundreds of gold and silver pieces in the 1st century

Puruchuco
Five-hundred-year-old cemetery where 10,000 Inca mummies were discovered

Kuélap Fortress
A pre-Inca fortress built between 1100 and 1300

ANDES MOUNTAINS

★ LIMA

BOLIVIA

Caral
Oldest city in the Americas; at least 4,000 years old

Cuzco

Lake Titicaca

N
W   E
S

KEY

🧵 Mummy Site

🌀 Nazca Drawings

🏛 Site of Ancient City

Nazca drawings
Large line drawings carved into the desert around 200

Pacific Ocean

Machu Picchu
Inca city built around 1430; best known archaeological site in Peru

CHILE

TIME
FOR KIDS

Trail of Tears

The Indian Removal Act of 1830 forced thousands of Cherokee people off their land.

The Trail of Tears

Defying the United States Supreme Court, President Andrew Jackson forced thousands of Cherokee people to leave their land.

The Granger Collection

▲ European settlers meet with Indians in what is now Georgia.

From the time that Europeans settled in North America, they were in conflict with the people who were already there, called American Indians. There were and are many different Indian Nations across the continent.

The Indian Removal Act

In 1828 the people of the Cherokee Nation lived in north Georgia. Their land was rich in gold. Members of the U.S. government wanted control of that wealth.

In 1830 Congress passed the Indian Removal Act. President Andrew Jackson signed the act, which would force the Cherokee off their land. Senators Daniel Webster and Davy Crockett fought for the Cherokee's rights.

Even the U.S. Supreme Court disagreed with President Jackson. The justices said that the Cherokee Nation was sovereign, meaning that it was a country. That meant that the U.S. Congress could not control the use of Cherokee land. The Cherokee would have to agree to their removal in a treaty. The treaty would then have to be ratified by the U.S. Senate.

In 1835 two members of the Cherokee tribe, Major Ridge and Elias Boudinot, signed a treaty that would remove the Cherokee from their land. Most of the Cherokee people disagreed, but the Senate ratified the treaty. It passed by just one vote.

Library of Congress/Prints and Photographs Division

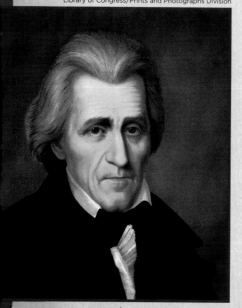

▲ Andrew Jackson

A painting of the Trail of Tears

The Granger Collection, New York

Nunna daul Tsuny

In 1838 the United States started moving the Cherokee people to Oklahoma. General John Wood, who was ordered to move the tribe, refused. He resigned in protest. But a replacement, General Winfield Scott, soon returned with 7,000 soldiers.

The U.S. Army forced 17,000 men, women, and children from their land. The Cherokees were herded into shelters and then forced to march 1,000 miles. They were short on food, blankets, and medicine. More than 4,000 people died along the way.

The route they traveled and the journey itself became known as the Trail of Tears. In Cherokee the name is Nunna daul Tsuny, meaning the trail where they cried.

Cherokee traditions are still alive. ▶

What Happened Next

Senator Davy Crockett lost his seat in Congress because he supported the Cherokee people. The Cherokee killed Major Ridge, his son, and Elias Boudinot.

The Cherokee land was available to gold prospectors. Soon they were everywhere. In 1849, when gold was discovered in California, the prospectors moved on, leaving ghost towns behind.

The Cherokee people, however, continued their traditions in Oklahoma. Today the people of the Cherokee Nation run schools, health programs, casinos, and more. They also keep alive the memory of those who suffered and died on the Trail of Tears.

Richard A. Cooke/Corbis

AMERICA IN 1850

The midpoint of the 19th century was a challenging time for the United States.

Pioneers headed west during the 1850s. ▶

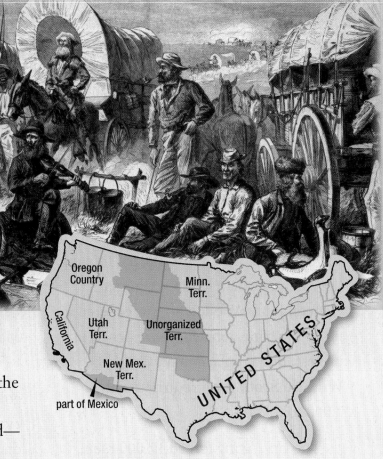

Corbis

▲ **States and territories, 1850**

America in 1850 was a complicated place. The eastern half of what is now the United States of America included free states—states where slavery was banned— and states where slavery was legal. Everything west of Iowa and Wisconsin was a territory and not yet included in the United States. Zachary Taylor was President.

In New England, writers were producing newspapers and literature. The *New York Times* newspaper was founded. Nathaniel Hawthorne's *The Scarlet Letter* was published.

In the Midwest, Kansas City was founded. Pioneering farmers still faced land disputes with Native Americans. New treaties clarified who owned which land.

Brigham Young, the founder of the Church of the Latter Day Saints (Mormons), had led his followers to Salt Lake City. There in the Utah territory the Mormons began to build their home.

In the West, the Gold Rush had brought thousands of people to California. Thousands more were moving to the Pacific Northwest from Missouri along the Oregon Trail. Pioneers were making their way to the Pacific coast, and the population was exploding.

INDUSTRY, AGRICULTURE, AND WAR

For Texas ranchers, the Gold Rush made California a good market for their cattle until about 1857. Cattle drives from south central Texas to San Francisco could take five to six months. Still, the drives were profitable. Within a few years, however, the price ranchers could get for their cattle dropped and the long drives largely stopped.

In 1850, more than 60 percent of the labor force in the United States was made up of farmers. Even so, the Industrial Revolution had taken hold in the Northeast. Coal and iron were plentiful. Factories and mills had plenty of jobs to offer and people moved to the cities in large numbers. Even children were employed in factories and mills in large numbers. Rivers, canals, and railroads were used to transport raw materials and manufactured goods from place to place.

▲Factories like these in New Jersey employed more and more workers in 1850.

At the same time, the economy of the South was largely still based on agriculture. Slave labor provided the necessary workforce and kept costs low.

The Civil War temporarily slowed westward migration. Cattle ranching in Texas and elsewhere in the Southwest was at a standstill during the war, but expanded rapidly again when the war ended. Farming and ranching expanded rapidly in the Midwest through the Great Plains where there was plenty of open land.

◀Enslaved workers, including children, provided a low-cost workforce in the South.

THE RAIL LINK BETWEEN EAST AND WEST

Talk of the need for a railroad to connect the East and West had started in the 1830s. Two routes were considered. Many planners supported the "central" route. This route would take the railroad westward through Nebraska, southern Wyoming, northern Utah and Nevada, across the Sierra Nevada to Sacramento, California.

Others, concerned about problems that might be caused by severe weather in the north, wanted the "southern" route. This route would travel through Texas and territory that belonged to Mexico before ending at Los Angeles. In order to have the route entirely within the United States, the government purchased southern portions of what are now New Mexico and Arizona for the railroad. Eventually, however, the central route was approved by Congress in 1862.

The work of laying the track for the railroad was done by thousands of immigrants from Ireland and China, as well as Civil War veterans from both the Union and Confederate armies. Over time, these immigrants, and immigrants from Scandinavia that settled in the Midwest, contributed to the cultural diversity of the young United States.

PEOPLE OF THE UNITED STATES— 1850 AND TODAY

There are 11 times more people in the United States today than there were in 1850. But about the same percentage of people were born here as were born abroad.

In 1850, more than 90 percent of immigrants came from Europe. Today only 23 percent of immigrants come from Europe. Instead, the majority come from Latin America and Asia. — *Lisa Jo Rudy*

Courtesy Central Pacific Railroad Photographic History Museum/CPRR.org

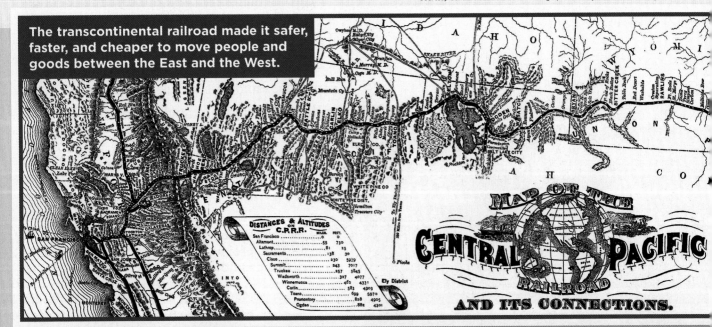

The transcontinental railroad made it safer, faster, and cheaper to move people and goods between the East and the West.

Chinese workers were among the thousands of immigrants who helped build the railroad.

Courtesy Central Pacific Railroad Photographic History Museum/CPRR.org

In the News in 1850

- The women's suffrage movement got started. Women started campaigning for the right to vote.
- I. M. Singer and Company patented the first sewing machine.
- P. T. Barnum brought singer Jenny Lind, the Swedish Nightingale, to America.

He advertised everywhere. She was met at the dock by 30,000 New Yorkers!

- Joel Houghton invented the first automatic dishwasher.
- Levi Strauss began making blue jeans.

The Granger Collection, New York

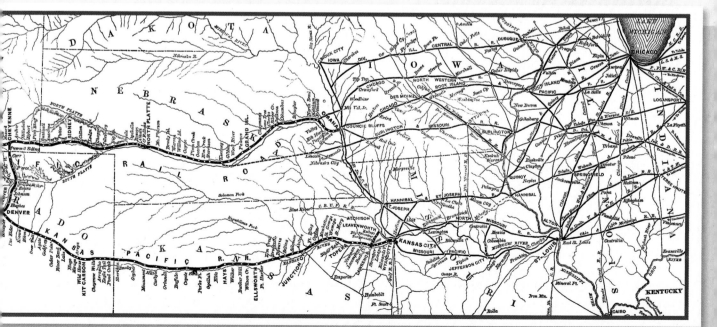

The Path to Independence

From the first European settlements onward, American history is the story of diverse people creating a new kind of nation and learning to live together. Here are some highlights:

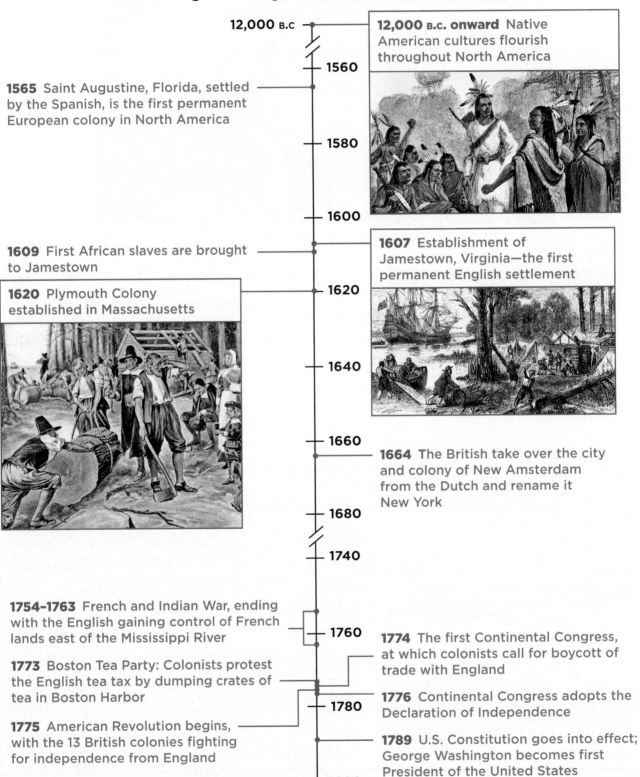

12,000 B.C

12,000 B.C. onward Native American cultures flourish throughout North America

1560

1565 Saint Augustine, Florida, settled by the Spanish, is the first permanent European colony in North America

1580

1600

1607 Establishment of Jamestown, Virginia—the first permanent English settlement

1609 First African slaves are brought to Jamestown

1620 Plymouth Colony established in Massachusetts

1620

1640

1660

1664 The British take over the city and colony of New Amsterdam from the Dutch and rename it New York

1680

1740

1754–1763 French and Indian War, ending with the English gaining control of French lands east of the Mississippi River

1760

1774 The first Continental Congress, at which colonists call for boycott of trade with England

1773 Boston Tea Party: Colonists protest the English tea tax by dumping crates of tea in Boston Harbor

1776 Continental Congress adopts the Declaration of Independence

1780

1775 American Revolution begins, with the 13 British colonies fighting for independence from England

1789 U.S. Constitution goes into effect; George Washington becomes first President of the United States

1800

TIME FOR KIDS

(c) AP Photo/Eric Gay; (tr) A. T. Willett/Alamy

A Happy Day in June

Honoring Our Diverse History

America's remarkable success is based on our willingness to respect our differences as well as value our common heritage.

Free to Celebrate

A key day in June marks the end of slavery—and the beginning of an important holiday for human rights.

By Anna Prokos

The Granger Collection, New York

On June 19, 1865, General Gordon Granger of the Union army sailed into Galveston's harbor. He delivered the good news that would change Texas forever. "The people of Texas are informed that, in accordance with a Proclamation from the Executive [President] of the United States, all slaves are free."

With this message, 250,000 African Americans were given new hope for the future. Slaves in Texas had waited more than two years to be given their freedom. This was true even though President Abraham Lincoln's Emancipation Proclamation had taken effect in 1863. Texans knew about Lincoln freeing slaves. But there weren't enough Union forces in the state to enforce the rules. Slaves in Texas were the last in the United States to gain their freedom.

One year after Granger's speech, African Americans all over Texas celebrated June 19. It was the beginning of the holiday called Juneteenth. Although ex-slaves were now allowed to work for wages, they did not have the same rights as whites. For example, they were not allowed to use the same parks as white citizens. This didn't stop African Americans from holding Juneteenth celebrations in parks. In fact, many African Americans in Austin, Houston, and Mexia raised enough money to buy their own park lands.

African Americans celebrate freedom on Juneteenth.

The Granger Collection, New York

A Juneteenth celebration in Tucson, Arizona

A Holiday for All

The annual celebrations became a symbol of African American culture. Soon neighboring states began holding Juneteenth celebrations too. They often included religious services, stories from former slaves, picnics, dancing, music, games, horse races, and sports.

Today, Juneteenth festivities are held throughout the United States and around the world. People of all races and nationalities come together to celebrate freedom and liberty. They pay tribute to history and changes in society. Juneteenth is an important day to honor human rights.

On June 1, 1979, a history-making law proclaimed June 19 a legal state holiday in Texas—113 years after the initial celebration. Juneteenth also became the first official African-American holiday in the United States. Today, many groups and government leaders are working to make Juneteenth a national holiday.

Grounds for Freedom

African Americans were not allowed to use parks designated for whites, but they needed a place to celebrate Juneteenth. Raising and collecting money to buy land wasn't an easy task for ex-slaves, but they did it. Today, Juneteenth celebrations are still held on or near these grounds.

Emancipation Park, Houston

History: Reverend Jack Yates helped to raise $1,000 to buy 10 acres of land. The land was named Emancipation Park.

Today: In 2007, the park became a protected historic landmark. The group Friends of Emancipation Park is working to restore the park. Their hope is to once again make the park the center of the surrounding communities.

Courtesy Dave Schafer/ City of Houston

Emancipation Park, East Austin

History: In 1872, freed slaves from Freedmen's Town paid $3,000 to purchase 10 acres of land. For decades, Emancipation Park was the only public park for African Americans in Austin.

Today: Juneteenth celebrations are held in Rosewood Park and throughout Austin.

Booker T. Washington Park, Mexia

History: In 1898, the Nineteenth of June Organization purchased this park for the cultural celebration. Early Juneteenth activities were often interrupted by white landowners who demanded that celebrators return to work. The park once hosted the state's largest Juneteenth celebration, with 20,000 African Americans joining in the festivities.

Today: Annual Juneteenth festivities are still celebrated here, and a historical marker at the entrance of the park tells about the history and significance of the area.

A Melting Pot

The people of Texas are the people of the world. *By Anna Prokos*

San Antonio's River Walk is a great place to sample the local culture.

William Manning/Corbis

Want to learn about different cultures? Just look around Texas! Because of its geography and history, Texas is a blend of world cultures and traditions. A recent U.S. Census identified at least 30 different ethnic groups living in the Lone Star State. Each group's traditions, foods, music, art, culture, and celebrations can be found in many areas. The cultural traditions and events Texans share are as diverse as the people themselves. Texans take pride in their state, but they also celebrate the world cultures that have shaped their lives.

Here First

Native American groups made up the state's early population. Archaeologists have found remains of Native American societies in Texas dating as far back as 12,000 years! Evidence of the Native American culture is still strong today. Many cities and parks have Native American names, including Comanche Crossing, which was the route of Comanche tribes as they migrated and settled in the area.

Today, three federally recognized tribes live in Texas. They continue to honor their cultural heritage through Powwows that draw tens of thousands of people. They enjoy traditional dances, stories, food, and music.

Other events highlight Native American culture. In Post, for example, an annual ceremony takes place the day after the first day of spring. A Plains Indian dance is performed for success of the year's crops. In October, downtown Dallas comes alive with traditional Native American costumes, music, and food at the American Indian Art Festival and Market.

Kevin R. Morris/Corbis

Native American culture has had a strong influence throughout Texas.

Settling the Land

In 1685, French explorers landed in Texas by mistake when they were on their way to find the mouth of the Mississippi River. Rene-Robert Cavelier, or La Salle, established a colony and began to build forts in the area. Texas soon became a French territory, and these European settlers built many churches and hospitals throughout the state.

After the French, Spanish settlers set their sights on Texas. They demanded that Native Americans adopt their culture and lifestyle. The group built missions, or churches and villages, to spread Spanish ideas throughout the state. The missions brought European livestock, fruits, vegetables, and goods to Texas. At one point, there were 26 missions in the state. Four of those missions can still be seen at San Antonio Missions National Park.

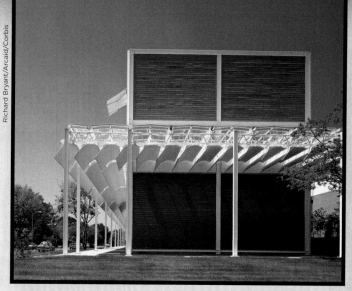
▲ The Menil Collection is a museum in Houston that was established by French art collectors John and Dominique de Menil.

▲ This painting by the famous French artist René Magritte is part of the Menil Collection.

Did you know?

The reverse side of the state seal of Texas displays each of the six national flags that have flown over the land throughout history. They are the Spanish flag, the French flag, the Mexican flag, the flag of the Republic of Texas, the flag of the U.S. Confederacy, and the flag of the United States of America.

◀ As more Mexican families move into southern Texas, cultures continue to blend together. Tex-Mex food and traditional Mexican celebrations, like Cinco de Mayo, give southern Texas its unique mix of Mexican cultures and American traditions.

Mark Gibson/Alamy

Mexican Influence

Texas shares a lengthy border with Mexico, so it's no wonder Mexican culture drifts into the state. In the late 1800s, Mexican and Spanish people, called Tejanos, established homes, churches, and schools throughout Texas.

In the 1820s and 1830s, Tejano groups set up large ranches to raise livestock and grow produce on fertile ground. They also had strong military plans to defend Mexico's northern frontier. During this time, Texas became an independent and self-governed land called Coahuila y Tejas.

Mexican national and religious holidays became large celebrations for Tejanos, especially Mexican Independence Day on September 16. The first celebration in 1835 lasted for three days. It included religious services, parades, and formal balls called fandangos. During Fandangos, celebrators wore colorful Mexican costumes to perform traditional dances. Today, Mexican Independence Day fiestas are held throughout San Antonio, El Paso, Houston, and Austin.

Did you know?

Texas was the first Mexican state settled by Anglo-Americans. The Anglos helped spread Tejano culture throughout the U.S. Tejano words like lasso and corral quickly reached the American West. So did the Tejanos' love of raising cattle. Their large cattle farms turned Texas into a major beef-producing state.

Battling for Land

In the early 1830s, Anglo-Americans began moving down into Texas from the United States. They clashed with Mexicans and battled over land. One of the most famous was the Battle of the Alamo. Some Tejanos sided with the Americans, others with the Mexicans. But many Texan and Tejano troops joined together in their fight against Mexican troops. They forced Mexican soldiers out of the Alamo, but were then attacked for 13 days by a growing number of Mexican soldiers.

After a bloody battle, 189 Texans and up to 600 Mexican fighters were dead. That led to the Battle of San Jacinto on April 21, 1836. Texans attacked Mexican forces, shouting, "Remember the Alamo!" They forced Mexican troops out of the area, and Texas once again became an independent republic. In 1845, Texas joined the United States.

An artist's rendering of the Battle of the Alamo ▼

The Granger Collection, New York

Celebrating Cultures

Festivities throughout the year celebrate Texas' cultural heritage. Here's a list of a few well-known celebrations.

February-March
- Charro Days, Brownsville
- North Texas Irish Festival, Dallas
- Borderfest, Hidalgo

April
- Fiesta, San Antonio
- Germanfest, Muenster
- Riofest, Harlingen
- Austin Celtic Festival, Austin

May
- National Polka Festival, Ennis
- Cinco de Mayo, around the state

June
- Juneteenth, throughout the state
- Texas Folklife Festival, San Antonio
- Texas Scottish Festival and Highland Games, Arlington

July
- Bluegrass Festival, Overton

August
- Blues Festival, Navasota

September
- Labor Day: West Fest, West
- September 16 Mexican Independence Day: San Antonio, El Paso, Houston, and Austin
- Medina Lake Cajun Festival, Medina Lake

October
- Oktoberfest, throughout the state to celebrate German heritage and culture
- October 25 Day of the Dead, Port Isabel
- Yorktown Western Days, Yorktown

November-December
- Wurstfest, New Braunfels
- Nine Flags Festival, Nacogdoches, the oldest town in Texas.
- George West Storyfest, George West

A Nation of Many Languages

This map shows the number (in millions) of people in the United States over 5 years of age who speak a language other than English at home. This information was gathered during the 2000 U.S. Census.

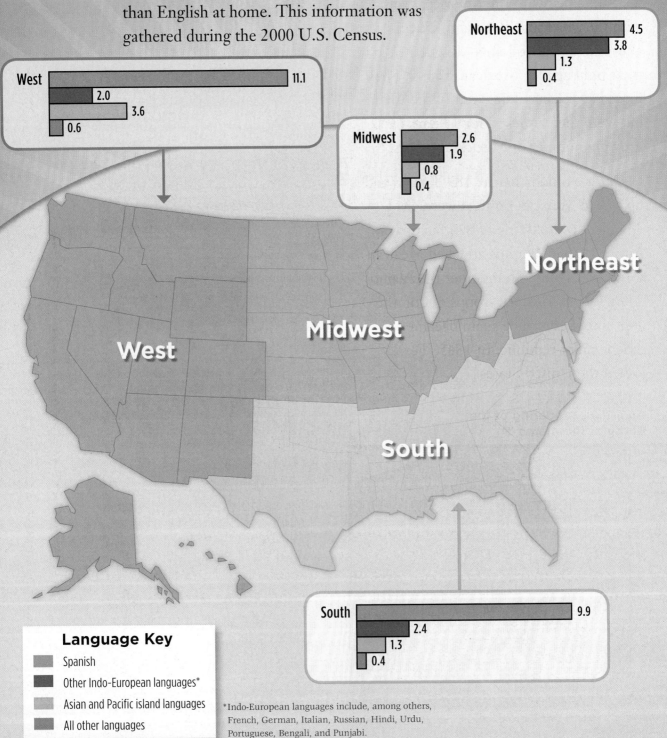

Northeast
- 4.5
- 3.8
- 1.3
- 0.4

West
- 11.1
- 2.0
- 3.6
- 0.6

Midwest
- 2.6
- 1.9
- 0.8
- 0.4

South
- 9.9
- 2.4
- 1.3
- 0.4

Northeast

West

Midwest

South

Language Key
- Spanish
- Other Indo-European languages*
- Asian and Pacific island languages
- All other languages

*Indo-European languages include, among others, French, German, Italian, Russian, Hindi, Urdu, Portuguese, Bengali, and Punjabi.

TIME FOR KIDS

Chasing El Niño

Technology helps scientists predict when the next El Niño may strike.

Why the West Is Burning

David McNew/Getty Images

Parts of the western United States have been experiencing severe drought conditions for a number of years.

Ethan Miller/Getty Images

Drought starts with a period of low rainfall. That causes the soil to dry up and plants to die. Water levels in rivers and lakes fall. Summers with little rain are followed by winters with little snow. Are current droughts in the West unusual, or are they part of a pattern that spans thousands of years?

▲ **The effects of an extended drought can be seen in the water level of Lake Meade at Hoover Dam.**

Tracking Centuries of Droughts

The Western United States is a semiarid region, marked with light rainfall. As such it is subject to periods of drought. Scientists are using tree-ring records to study the long-term pattern of droughts there. The rings of years when the tree received enough moisture are wide. The rings of years when it did not are narrow. Scientists have found that severe droughts centered on the Southwest happen, on average, twice each century. But what could trigger droughts that last for decades and even centuries? The Pacific weather patterns called El Niño and La Niña appear to be the most likely culprits. There is evidence that these tropical events are mirrored in other parts of the Pacific.

▼ **Tree rings show periods of drought as well as periods when water was plentiful.**

Peter Ryan/Photo Researchers

Rain and Drought Contribute to Forest Fires

Droughts dry forests out and turn undergrowth into kindling. But the most dangerous fires occur when droughts follow years that are unusually wet. That's because generous rains encourage trees, shrubs, and grasses to grow. The new growth provides more fuel to stoke forest fires in dry years.

Drought conditions fanned by energy imbalances in the ocean mean that perhaps the West will go on burning with no end in sight. — *Susan Moger*

Fires like this one are one of the more devastating consequences of drought. ▶

David McNew/Getty Images

Energy Changes That Affect Drought

Name	How It Affects Weather Patterns	Effects on Land	Cycle
El Niño	Rising water temperatures in the tropical Pacific Ocean upset the energy balance in the atmosphere, affecting ocean currents and storm patterns.	Changes normal rainfall patterns; can cause severe flooding in some places and severe drought in others	Three to seven years; more frequently with global warming
La Niña	Cooler water temperatures affect currents and storms.	Severe effects around the world; brings drought to some areas	Follows the El Niño cycle
North Pacific Temperatures	Sea surface temperatures in the North Pacific show warming and cooling patterns, affecting atmospheric pressure.	Affects storm paths in North America	Every 20 to 30 years
North Atlantic Warming and Cooling	If the North Atlantic warms at the same time as the Pacific Ocean, there is less rain in summer. If the ocean cools at the same time, there is less snow in winter.	Sets the stage for 1930s-Dust Bowl-style drought	N/A
Excess Greenhouse Gases	Excess greenhouse gases change the temperature of the atmosphere and oceans worldwide by trapping the sun's heat.	Could be responsible for rising ocean levels, more powerful storms, and changes in weather patterns	Continuous

Who Is This El Niño Anyway?

AP Photo/Reed Saxon

Warming or cooling of ocean water near the equator can change the weather and cause problems around the world.

El Niño means "child" in Spanish. It's also the name given to the periodic warming of the Pacific Ocean around the equator. It got its name because it usually appears in December, around the time many people celebrate the birth of Christ. La Niña is a cooling pattern that hits the same areas of the Pacific Ocean.

Anything that changes the weather can be an extremely big deal. The giant El Niño of 1997–98 ran its course for eight months. It killed about 2,100 people and caused at least $33 billion in property damage.

Flooding like this could be traced to the effects of El Niño. ▼

Rich Pedroncelli/Wide World Photo/AP Images

▲ **In Peru, rushing water from too much rain swept away homes and roads.**

El Niño Strikes

The El Niño pattern of the late 1990s was especially hard on Peru. Rain poured down for months, sometimes as much as 6 inches a day. Rivers overflowed. Farmers' fields, roads, and houses were destroyed. Pools of water became breeding grounds for malaria-causing mosquitoes.

Meanwhile, terrible droughts and ferocious heat hit Indonesia. Forest fires burned out of control. In the United States, mudslides and flash floods struck communities from California to Mississippi. Terrible storms hit the Gulf Coast. Tornadoes tore through Florida.

Then La Niña hit. Where there were floods, now there was drought. Where weather had been too warm, now it was terribly cold.

Heavy rains from El Niño caused landslides along the coast and in the mountains. ▼

How El Niño Works

Ordinarily, trade winds blow west over the Pacific. They warm the surface of the water. Meanwhile, all along the eastern Pacific, colder water comes up from under the surface.

El Niño changes all that. Suddenly—no one really knows why—the trade winds switch off. Without the trade winds, the water doesn't move. It just gets hotter and hotter, finally evaporating and coming down as torrential rain in places like California. So much freshwater rain affects the saltiness of the sea. Ocean animals die. Fishermen can't find enough fish, or they find only warm-water fish that usually live in other places.

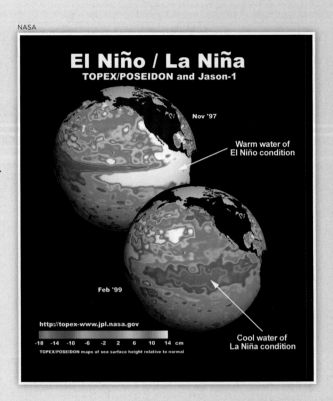

El Niño / La Niña
TOPEX/POSEIDON and Jason-1

Nov '97

Warm water of
El Niño condition

Feb '99

http://topex-www.jpl.nasa.gov

-18 -14 -10 -6 -2 2 6 10 14 cm
TOPEX/POSEIDON maps of sea surface height relative to normal

Cool water of
La Niña condition

Predicting the Weather

To predict when and how El Niño and La Niña will strike, governments now use high-tech buoys anchored in the Pacific. These buoys are an early warning system for El Niño. Scientists also use superfast computers to create models of the climate.

These tools help scientists predict when the next El Niño cycle will strike. They are even starting to predict exactly what kind of weather changes to expect as El Niño and La Niña change the way the wind blows. — *Lisa Jo Rudy*

A technician checks one of the high-tech buoys that can provide early warnings of changing weather patterns. ▼

Twister Time

Under the right conditions, a thunderstorm can turn into a tornado. A tornado is a rotating funnel-shaped cloud that contains winds that can blow up to 299 miles per hour. During El Niño tornadoes may be more likely to take place in the states bordering the Gulf of Mexico and in central Florida. This is because the winter sea surface temperature is warmer than usual. During La Niña tornadoes are more likely to happen in the upper Midwest and southeastern Texas. This is caused by cooler temperatures.

Top 5
Deadliest Tornadoes in the United States

Date	Location	Deaths
1. March 18, 1925	Tri-State (Illinois, Indiana, and Missouri)	695
2. May 6, 1840	Natchez, Mississippi	317
3. May 27, 1896	St. Louis, Missouri	255
4. April 5, 1936	Tupelo, Mississippi	216
5. April 6, 1936	Gainesville, Georgia	203

Did you know?

Almost half of all tornadoes fall into the F1, or moderate damage category. These tornadoes can overturn automobiles and uproot trees.

Fujita Scale
The Fujita scale classifies tornadoes according to the damage they cause.

Scale	Wind Speed (miles per hour)	Possible Damage
F0	42–72 mph	Light
F1	73–112 mph	Moderate
F2	113–157 mph	Significant
F3	158–207 mph	Severe
F4	208–260 mph	Devastating
F5	261–318 mph	Incredible

Getty Images

A Bird Came Down the Walk

By Emily Dickinson

A Bird came down the Walk—
He did not know I saw—
He bit an Angleworm in halves
And ate the fellow, raw,

And then he drank a Dew
From a convenient Grass—
And then hopped sidewise to the Wall
To let a Beetle pass—

He glanced with rapid eyes
That hurried all around—
They looked like frightened Beads, I thought—
He stirred his Velvet Head

Like one in danger, Cautious,
I offered him a Crumb
And he unrolled his feathers
And rowed him softer home—

Than Oars divide the Ocean,
Too silver for a seam—
Or Butterflies, off Banks of Noon
Leap, plashless as they swim.

TIME ·FOR· KIDS

Protecting Our Rights

The Power of the Constitution

The U.S. Constitution is the foundation for our government and allows us to respond to changing times.

Equal Rights for All

Many brave people have stood up for what they believe in. Thanks to their courage, our nation has changed and moved forward—and continues to do so today.

By Anna Prokos

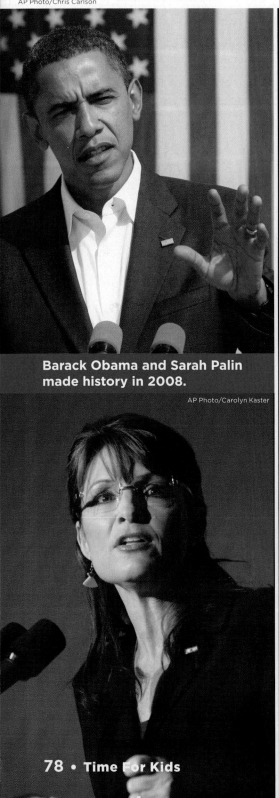

Barack Obama and Sarah Palin made history in 2008.

The presidential election of 2008 was historical in several ways, including the race and gender of the presidential teams. Barack Obama was the first African American nominated for president by a major political party. Sarah Palin was the first woman to run on the Republican presidential ticket. But what really made history was that Barack Obama became the first African American elected President of the United States.

Today, all people can be leaders in our government. But until the early 1900s, African Americans and women weren't allowed to hold public office. They couldn't even vote.

Women's Work

When Elizabeth Cady Stanton and Susan B. Anthony met in 1851, they formed a strong friendship—and a strong fight for women's rights. In the 1800s, women were not allowed to go to college. They couldn't own property. The only way to change these rules, Stanton and Anthony believed, was to grant suffrage—the right to vote—to women.

Although Anthony and Stanton worked tirelessly, they died before women were given voting rights in 1920. Their hard work was just the beginning of other equal rights movements.

Civil Rights

Slavery was abolished in 1865. But through the 1950s, African Americans were treated unfairly. They were not allowed to go to the same schools or public places as whites.

A group of parents in Topeka, Kansas, tried to register their children in an all-white school in 1954. When the kids were denied, the parents went to the courts. This historical case was called Brown vs. Board of Education of the City of Topeka, KS. The court decided that all citizens should have the same rights to equal education. It was one of the first steps for the Civil Rights Movement.

Months later, in Montgomery, Alabama, Rosa Parks refused to move to the back of the bus for a white rider. She was arrested. Martin Luther King, Jr., organized a bus boycott. People refused to ride buses in Montgomery and around the nation. The boycott lasted for 381 days. Finally, the Supreme Court ruled that segregation in public transportation was illegal.

An estimated 250,000 people attended the historic March on Washington, August 1963.

In 1960, four African Americans sat at a whites-only counter to order lunch. They were refused service, but the men sat peacefully until the store closed. They showed up again the next day, and the next. By the third day, there were 1,000 protesters at the store. These sit-ins spread across the country. Finally, the Civil Rights Act stated that public areas could no longer be divided according to race.

Thanks to brave people and courageous acts, our nation continues to move forward. Today, many people continue to work hard to make sure all citizens are treated fairly.

Arrested for Voting

Susan B. Anthony believed she had the right to vote because, according to the Constitution, she was a citizen. Citizens were allowed to vote, so she voted in the 1872 presidential election. Two weeks later, she was arrested. At the trial, the judge declared her guilty of illegal voting. He ordered her to pay $100 plus the cost of the trial. Anthony responded: "May it please your honor, I shall never pay a dollar of your unjust penalty." And she never did.

Susan B. Anthony (left) and Elizabeth Cady Stanton

It's Our Constitutional Right!

Our country's Constitution maps out how our government is run. But this document isn't stuck in the past—it changes with the times.

By Anna Prokos

"We, the people of the United States, in order to form a more perfect Union, establish justice, insure domestic tranquility, provide for the common defense, promote the general welfare, and secure the blessings of liberty to ourselves and our posterity, do ordain and establish this Constitution for the United States of America."

Those famous words mark the beginning, or preamble, to the U.S. Constitution. Our nation's founding fathers established the Constitution in 1787. They wanted the document to act as the "law of the land." The Constitution gives U.S. citizens freedoms and liberties—especially the Bill of Rights. The Bill of Rights outlines the first ten amendments to the Constitution. Amendments are additions to the original document. The Bill of Rights gives Americans the freedom of speech, freedom of religion, and many other rights we expect in our democracy.

The U.S. government is a democracy, which means our country's founding fathers envisioned a free society for the nation's people. The Constitution was created to ensure that the democracy succeeds.

Keeping It In Check

The Constitution breaks down the government into three major areas: legislative, executive, and judicial. These branches make certain that one area of government doesn't have major power over another. Each branch has equal footing when it comes to making laws. This is called checks and balances, and it's one way the U.S. government differs from other democracies.

The legislative branch consists of Congress. Congress has two parts: the Senate and the House of Representatives. Members of Congress are elected by people in each state. If voters don't like what Congress is doing, they have the chance to elect a new representative.

The executive branch is led by the President. The head of the U.S. government acts as Commander in Chief to the armed forces. The President also appoints members of the Cabinet and oversees all departments of the federal government. The President and Congress try to work together to pass laws. Sometimes these two branches agree, and sometimes they don't. This ensures that neither the President nor Congress has the ultimate power.

The judicial branch is headed up by the Supreme Court of the United States. This branch consists of the Chief Justice and eight Associate Justices. These judges hear cases that challenge laws and the Constitution. They figure out if something is a constitutional right. The President appoints the justices and the Senate confirms them.

Elected officials gather for session at the U.S. House of Representatives located in the Washington, D.C.

Working Together

How do the three branches work together? In many ways. For example, when a law needs to be passed, all branches have to weigh in on the matter. Congress votes on whether or not to pass the law. The President may veto, or reject, a law from Congress. But Congress can then vote to pass the law anyway. The judiciary branch interprets the laws that may be challenged by the people or by states. This system of checks and balances is one of the most important parts of the Constitution.

So is the Constitution's ability to change with the times. Throughout history, thousands of amendments have been proposed. But ratifying an amendment is a serious matter. In order for an amendment to pass, two-thirds of the House of Representatives and the Senate have to approve it. Then, the amendment gets sent to the states for approval. If three-fourths of the states authorize the amendment, it gets ratified, or added to the Constitution. Since the Constitution was adopted in 1787, only 27 amendments have been approved.

The Constitution may change over time, but some things will always remain the same. Just as the country's founding fathers intended more than 220 years ago, the Constitution of the United States will protect citizens and make sure our government remains a democracy.

Alex Wong/Getty Images

▲ **The original document of the Constitution of the United States is on display at the National Archives and Records Administration in Washington, D.C.**

Changing with the Times

Since the Constitution was adopted in 1787, it has been amended 27 times. Here's a look at some important amendments.

Amendment	What It Does	When It Was Ratified
13th	Abolishes slavery	1865
15th	Ensures that a citizen cannot be denied the right to vote based on race, color, or previous status as a slave	1870
19th	Gives women the right to vote	1920
22nd	Limits the President to two terms of 4 years each	1951
26th	Establishes the voting age as 18	1971

What Does the Constitution Say?

These topics often make news headlines today. All branches of government, as well as the people of the U.S., try to make sense of these important issues by looking at the Constitution.

Michael Siluk/Index Stock Imagery/Photolibrary

Students do not give up their right of free speech when they are on school grounds.

The Issue	The Question	The Problem	The Outcome
Students and Free Speech	Are students on the property of public schools guaranteed the right of free speech?	In 2007, the Supreme Court decided a case about a student who was suspended for holding up a sign outside a school. The sign said nothing illegal, but school officials said that its content was unacceptable.	The court agreed with the school but added, "While the court has limited student free speech rights in the past, young people do not give up all their First Amendment rights when they enter a school."
Immigration	Does everyone who lives in the U.S. get the same rights and freedoms?	Immigration is on the rise. Some people come to the United States legally and some live in the country illegally for a long time. Many illegal immigrants own businesses and have children that were born in the U.S. If illegal immigrants are caught, they face the risk of being sent out of the country.	The 14th Amendment, ratified in 1868, defines U.S. citizens as "all persons born or naturalized in the United States."
Habeas Corpus, the right for detainees to question why they're being held.	Do people held by the U.S. government in foreign jails have the right to question the reasons they are held?	In 2006, Congress passed the Military Commissions Act. The Act said that suspected terrorists held in prisons outside the U.S. by the U.S. military don't have the right to question why they're being detained.	Federal courts defended the Act, but the Supreme Court disagreed. Their decision showed that foreign prisoners held by the U.S. military have Habeas Corpus rights. They have a right to challenge or question their imprisonment.

How We Elect a PRESIDENT

Presidential election campaigns last a long time. **Here's why.**

1 Candidates decide they want to run for President. They announce their intention to run. Then they start campaigning—advertising, making public appearances, participating in debates. Candidates usually run for the nomination of one of the two major parties: Democratic or Republican.

2 State primary elections are held. People in each state vote for the candidates. The candidate from each party with the most votes from all the primaries usually becomes the party's nominee.

3 Each party holds a nominating convention. At this meeting, held over several days, the party officially chooses its candidate.

4 The candidates campaign more—describing their positions, debating, and trying to convince citizens to vote for them.

5 On election day, which is always the first Tuesday in November, eligible voters exercise their right to vote.

6 The candidate with the majority of electoral votes wins. A state's electoral votes are based on the number of representatives that state has in Congress. Candidates receive electoral votes based on the popular vote—how many people in the state voted for them.

7 On January 20 of the following year, the new President of the United States takes office.

TIME FOR KIDS

Lights Out!

Eclipses turn day into night.

Catch a Comet by Its Tail

A space capsule captures evidence of cosmic history and brings it back to Earth.

The space capsule blazed through the skies at 30,000 miles per hour. Nearing Earth, it was slowed by parachutes. Then it landed safely in a Utah desert. The capsule was from space mission *Stardust,* and it carried a special cargo. On board was the first material ever collected from a comet.

What Are Comets?

Comets are chunks of ice, rock, and dust that are billions of years old. The comets we see from Earth come from a region called the Kuiper Belt. It is located just outside the orbit of Neptune. These comets orbit the sun in 200 years or less. When one gets close to the sun, we can see it from Earth.

Surprising Stardust Images

Stardust took close-up images of the comet Wild 2 (pronounced "vilt") from about 150 miles away.

The Stardust capsule streaked through Earth's atmosphere and landed in the Utah desert. ▼

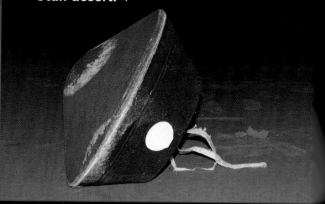

The images of the comet's core, "a dirty snowball" made of dust and ice, surprised NASA scientists. "We were amazed by the feature-rich surface of the comet," says Donald Brownlee of the University of Washington. "There are barn-size boulders, 100-meter high cliffs, and some weird terrain unlike anything we've ever seen before."

NASA

Closeup of a comet ▶

Precious Particles

Five years after its 1999 launch, *Stardust* flew to within 150 miles of Comet 81P/Wild 2. *Stardust* stuck out a tennis-racket-like contraption to catch tiny grains of material being blown off the surface of the comet. The microscopic particles were put in aerogel, an airy goo. Aerogel is so light, it has been described as frozen smoke. The aerogel kept the comet particles safe for the trip to Earth.

Why is this so exciting? Comets are like cosmic time capsules. They contain material that has been in the deep freeze for more than 4.5 billion years. By looking at comet particles, scientists can get information about how the solar system formed.

Volunteers at Work

After the particles packed in aerogel arrived on Earth, scientists used a scanning microscope to collect digital images of the aerogel contents. These images were made available to volunteer scientists around the world.

Volunteers had to pass a test given on the *Stardust* mission Web page. One scientist compared the task to searching for ants on a football field. Once particles were located, researchers carefully extracted the dust to analyze it. As a reward, the volunteers who located grains of space dust got to name them!

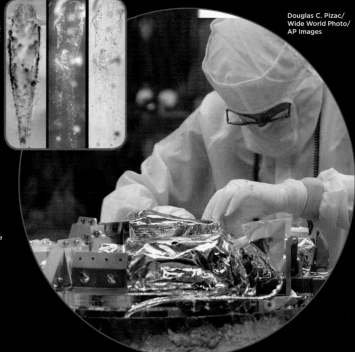

NASA

Douglas C. Pizac/
Wide World Photo/
AP Images

▲ A researcher retrieves cosmic dust.

Something New in the Universe

"A portion of the organic material in the samples is unlike anything seen before," says Scott Sandford, a NASA scientist. "People will be working on these samples for decades to come," he said. In terms of their scientific value, he continued, the particles are "a gift that keeps on giving."

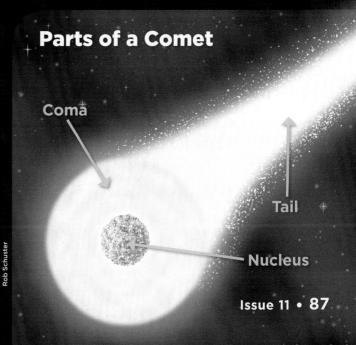

Parts of a Comet

Coma

Tail

Nucleus

Rob Schuster

LOOK! Up in the Sky!

Scientists shed light on eclipses.

By Andrea Delbanco

In Ghana a school group gathers to stare at the sky.

On March 29, 2006, people across the world gazed at the sky to watch a total eclipse of the sun. The area of total darkness began in eastern Brazil and traveled across the Atlantic Ocean. Next it crossed northern Africa, the Mediterranean region, Turkey, and finally central Asia. In each place along the path, the sun disappeared for just a few minutes and the sky turned dark. Birds stopped singing, and it was as if night had suddenly fallen. Then in each place, just as suddenly, the sun reappeared.

A total solar eclipse happens when the orbits of the sun, the moon, and Earth line up exactly. The moon passes in front of the sun and blocks it out while the shadow of the moon travels across Earth. The area in the shadow is called the totality, and being in one can be an amazing experience.

In Egypt a visitor to the pyramids gets a view of the eclipse.

"A total eclipse is one of those experiences that make you feel like you're part of the larger universe," said one eclipse viewer, NASA scientist Janet Luhmann.

What Happened to the Sun?

A total eclipse is possible because of a coincidence. The moon and the sun look to be about the same size in the sky. That's in spite of the fact that the sun is much bigger than the moon. In fact, a total of 400 moons could line up side by side along the sun's diameter. So how can the two objects appear to be the same size? The answer is that the sun is about 400 times farther away than the moon. Those two facts together mean that the moon is just big enough to block out the sun—but only when they line up just right.

During an eclipse the round disk of the moon appears as a black circle over the sun. Slowly the circle of the moon moves across the sun until it blocks it out completely. It keeps moving until the sun begins to appear on the other side. The whole event takes about three hours from start to finish. But the time of total darkness is just a few minutes.

The area of the totality, or total darkness, during an eclipse is relatively small. Usually it is about 150 miles in diameter. Outside of the totality, there is an area of lesser shadow, where viewers can see a partial eclipse. It appears as though the sun is partially covered by the disk of the moon. During a partial eclipse, the sky darkens a little, like at twilight.

Nicolas Postal/AFP/Getty Images

In Niger a West African man wears solar shades.

◄ **In Pakistan students protect their eyes with strips of X-ray film.**

Khalid Tanveer/Wide World Photo/AP Images

Two Types of Solar Eclipses

There are two types of solar eclipses. The total eclipse is when the orbit of the moon is not a perfect circle. Its distance from Earth can vary by thousands of miles. A total eclipse occurs when the sun and the moon line up and the moon is at its closest to Earth. The moon casts two shadows. In the small shadow, called an umbra, the sun is totally blacked out. In the larger penumbra area, people see a partial eclipse. They are able to see part of the top or bottom of the sun.

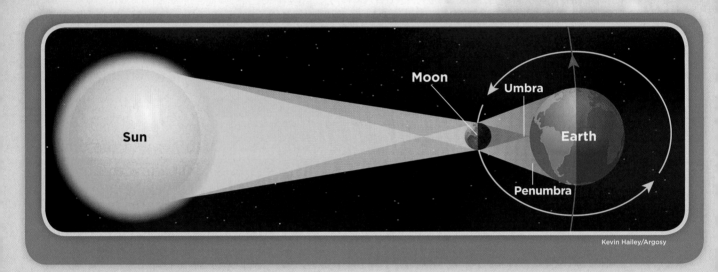

Kevin Hailey/Argosy

An annular eclipse is when the sun and the moon line up, but the moon is at its farthest point from Earth, and the disk of the moon is too small to completely cover the sun. During an annular eclipse, a ring of the sun is still visible around the disk of the moon. The bright ring is called an annulus.

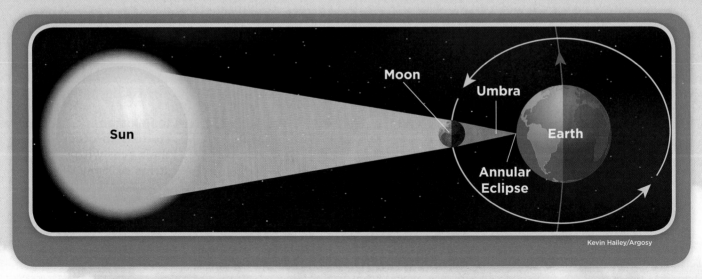

Kevin Hailey/Argosy

Viewing Eclipses Safely

Take some steps to ensure your safety when viewing an eclipse. Looking at the sun can seriously damage your eyes. Never look directly at the sun, not with your naked eye and especially not with a telescope or binoculars.

The safest and easiest way to observe an eclipse is with a pinhole camera, because you are not looking directly at the sun. Also, when using protective lenses, make sure the lenses are safe for viewing eclipses.

Make Your Plans Now

Scientists, amateur astronomers, and tourists plan years ahead to be in the right place for a solar eclipse. The dates of future eclipses have been plotted out for the next century, so you can take your pick. Will you be going to the Faroe Islands in March 2015?

Too far to go? If you can wait, there will be a total eclipse of the sun visible across much of the United States on August 21, 2017, and another on April 8, 2024. Make your travel plans now!

Viorgos Karahalis/Reuters/Newscom

Corona Mystery

Eclipses aren't just spectacular to watch. They also give scientists a chance to study the sun's corona. The corona is the outermost layer of the sun's atmosphere, and it is only visible during a total eclipse. The corona holds one of the mysteries of the sun. Although the sun's surface is about 11,000 degrees Fahrenheit, the corona is much hotter—almost 2 million degrees.

This map shows the path of the 2006 solar eclipse. Many scientists traveled along this path to observe the corona effect. ▶

The Poet Stumbles Upon the Astronomer's Orchards

By Nancy Willard

Once a scholar showed me the sky.
He held up a grapefruit:
here is the sun.
He held up an orange:
this is the harvest moon.
If you watch my hands, you will see
how the sun stays in its socket,
how the earth turns, how the moon
ripens and falls and swells again.

Under an axle tree, I took my seat.
The leaves were stars,
      juggling pineapples and pears.
        What a show!
A thousand lemons are rolling through space,
avocados nudge down the rings of Jupiter
and coconuts shake the galaxy to its teeth
till the tree loses its leaves.

But there is a star in my apple when I cut it
and some hungry traveler is paring the moon away.

TIME FOR KIDS

Spend or Save?

It's never too soon to learn how to manage your money.

VIRTUAL MILLIONS

Kids learn about free enterprise.

Marianna Day Massey/Zuma/Corbis

▲ **The New York Stock Exchange is located on Wall Street in New York City.**

The United States economy is based on free enterprise—an economic system in which people have the freedom to own property and businesses and can decided what to make, how much to produce, and what price to charge. Free enterprise is based on supply and demand. It is part of a system of global interdependence among nations that allows countries to exchange goods. Every day people participate in free enterprise as they earn incomes, pay taxes, and budget and spend their money.

How would you like to have $100,000 to invest in free enterprise? It could happen to you—if your school takes part in a stock market competition. The contests are played by thousands of students in 16 states, from Florida to Hawaii. In the contest teams of three to five students are given $100,000 to invest in the stock market. They have ten weeks to see if they can earn more money than the other teams.

Stockbrokers use computers to follow the price of shares for their clients.

Ed Kashi/Corbis

Of course, the $100,000 isn't real. The dollars are simulated, or fake. The stock market is also simulated. Students trade on special Web sites run by stock-trading companies or by universities. Everything else about this contest is for real. First, teams pick real stocks that are being traded in real markets. Then, they follow the rise and fall of their picks in the real world. In the end the winning team is the one whose stocks make the most money.

Learning by Doing

Students like the games because they are an exciting way to learn. The dollars may not be real, but players experience the same feelings as an actual investor.

"We really think these kinds of interactive activities are great for the kids," said Chuck Wentz, a teacher at Fairland High School in Proctorville, Ohio. "Instead of just taking notes and taking tests, this gives students an idea of what really goes on," he added.

Students who take part in these contests understand that companies raise money by selling shares of stocks. Students realize that owning stock means owning a small piece of the company that issues the shares. How much a share costs depends on supply and demand. If many people want to buy a stock, its price will go up. On the other hand, if many people want to sell the stock, its value will go down. When many stock prices fall at once, it is often a sign of a weakening economy. Students must follow the ups and downs of their stocks and check news reports for anything that might affect their investments. In real life some people use a computer to buy and sell stocks, just as the students do. But many people also use stockbrokers to purchase stocks for them.

Studies have shown that many kids don't know how the stock market works. Learning about the stock market is important. Games that teach kids about the stock market are a great way to learn. You can buy and sell thousands of dollars worth of stocks—and all without risking a cent!

Sizing Up Stocks

A stock market table gives you basic information on a company's stock performance. You can use the table to learn how a stock's price is doing now or to review how it performed in the past. Here are some basic terms you should know when reading a stock table.

52 Week High and Low	Stock	Sales 100s	High	Low	Last	Chg
52.66	XYZ	81973	46.26	24.14	25.73	-0.08

52 Week High and Low
The highest and lowest prices paid for the stock over the past year.

Stock Symbol
This symbol represents the name of the company. It is usually similar to the company's name.

Sales 100s
This is the total amount of stocks traded on the previous day. The number is given in hundreds, so you will need to add 2 zeros to get the actual number of shares traded.

High
The highest price paid for the stock on the previous day the stock traded.

Low
The lowest price paid for the stock on the previous day the stock traded.

Last
Sometimes called the closing price, the last price paid for the stock at the end of the previous day.

Change
The difference between the last trade of the day and the previous day's price. A "-" stands for a negative change.

Bill Aaron/PhotoEdit

Money Counts

Teaching kids the value of a dollar

◀ **By spending their own money, kids learn about finance.**

P arents and children regularly face the challenges of money. Common topics include setting an allowance, learning to save, and deciding on expensive purchases. The goal of most parents is to teach their kids how to handle money wisely. The goal of most kids is getting money to spend. How can families balance these goals?

"All parents hope they'll raise a money-savvy kid, who'll grow up to be a financially secure adult," says financial planner Peg Eddy. The trick, say Eddy and most experts, is letting kids learn by having a little money of their own. They will also find it empowering.

The Tidler family in Denver found the best way to teach about money was to let their kids earn some. Their son, Ryan, 17, has been mowing lawns since he was 8. Now he owns his own equipment. He has been able to save $7,800. In addition, Ryan bought a dirt bike and an impressive sound system. Ryan doesn't resent having to make his own money when other kids are given cash by their parents. "Some kids have a lot of stuff," he says. "Some kids don't have much."

David Young-Wolff/PhotoEdit

Learn Now, Save Later

Money skills are an important part of becoming a successful adult. David Brady manages a mutual fund geared toward children and young adults. "Today we have debates about Social Security and pension plans dying out," he says. "These young people will have much more responsibility for their financial future than past generations."

Brady does caution kids. "They shouldn't be consumed with money," he says. However, they should understand basic principles for earning, saving, and investing.

That knowledge is greatly needed. Over the past decade, the average credit card debt of Americans ages 18 to 24 doubled, to nearly $3,000. Among high school seniors, four out of five have never taken a personal-finance class. On the other hand, nearly half have an ATM debit card, and more than a quarter have bounced a check.

PhotoLink/
Getty Images

Paying Off Credit Card Debt

Not paying off your credit card bill on time can be a bummer. The problem is, you have to pay interest on what you owe. This table is for an imaginary credit card. It shows how much it costs to pay off a debt, depending on what percentage of the balance you decide to pay each month. It also shows how much total money you must pay, including the interest, and how long it takes to pay it off.

Balance	Interest Rate	Payment	Payment	Total Payment	Debt Payoff
$2,000	18.90%	2%	$40	$7,820	30 years
$2,000	18.90%	4%	$80	$3,206	9 years, 8 months
$2,000	18.90%	6%	$120	$2,680	6 years, 2 months
$2,000	18.90%	8%	$160	$2,474	4 years, 7 months
$2,000	18.90%	10%	$200	$2,364	3 years, 9 months

Comstock Images

Talking About It

Contrary to what some parents think, many kids want to learn how to handle their money. They know they are being hit by constant consumer messages. They are also aware of the high cost of a college education.

Parents sometimes make the mistake when talking about money of discussing it only in terms of what kids shouldn't do. Instead, experts say, knowing how to handle money is the best way for kids to get what they really want. That means long-term planning and saving for big expenses like college or a car or even the annual holiday list. It also means thinking of others, by making donations to charity.

Giselle Lopez, 17, of New York City, learned the hard way. She racked up $2,000 in debt on her first credit card. Her parents refused to pay, so Giselle got a job. Then she paid the debt off slowly herself. "Now every time I use it, I know that it comes from my own pocket," Giselle says. "That gives me a sense of responsibility for my actions."

Different kids will have different styles when it comes to money. Teaching them how to use money doesn't have to mean setting rigid rules. When children like Ryan and Giselle have their own cash to consider, they can learn to set those rules themselves.

A credit card can send teens into debt. ▼

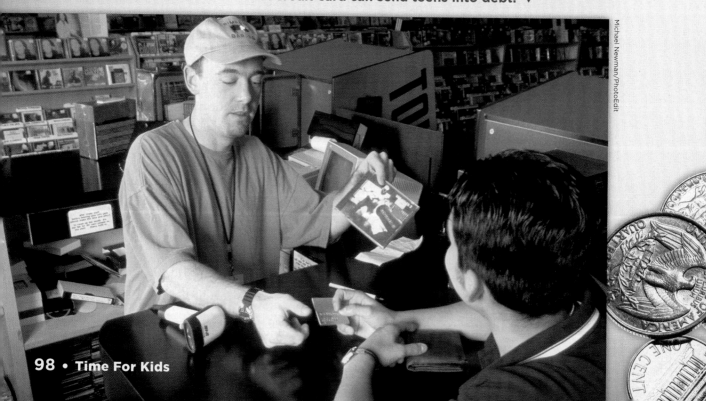

Michael Newman/PhotoEdit

The Money Game

There's finally a way for kids to learn the ins and outs of saving money. And best of all, it isn't a boring class—it's a game. There are online role-playing video games that teach teens and young adults the basics of managing money.

Here's an example of one game scenario. Players travel around the virtual game world, plunking down virtual cash at places like the mall or a car-rental agency. They earn spending money by taking quizzes. Sample question: What does APR stand for?

A) account percentage rate

B) average parcel rate

C) American paper route

D) annual percentage rate

For choosing D, you get $15 plus 10 percent interest each day on your virtual savings account.

No computer program can teach teens everything they need to know about the world of money, but it's a start.

(bkgd) Brian Hagiwara/Brand X Pictures/Getty Images

Teens with Checkbooks

- Fully 80 percent of high school seniors have opened bank accounts, and more than a quarter have bounced a check.

- Putting aside funds for the future is not a teen priority. One in four seniors say they rarely save at all, and only 17 percent describe themselves as thrifty.

- Credit card spending is rising. One third of seniors use plastic, either theirs or their parents'.

Kids should know how to keep track of the money they spend. ▶

Tony Freeman/PhotoEdit

Average Allowance

This table shows the average weekly allowances for kids, based on a survey done by Kids' Money. Of the adults who responded, 74 percent said that they give allowances. In addition, the survey found that many parents give all their children the same amount of allowance no matter what age the kids are. Some even give allowances to children who are in their 20s—and one 32-year-old was still getting an allowance!

Age	Average Allowance	Boys	Girls
4	$2.85	$2.48	$3.29
5	$3.15	$3.03	$3.27
6	$3.85	$3.32	$3.99
7	$4.10	$4.12	$4.07
8	$4.32	$4.45	$4.12
9	$5.52	$5.33	$5.71
10	$7.18	$6.56	$7.83
11	$7.92	$6.80	$9.07
12	$9.58	$9.38	$9.85
13	$9.52	$9.95	$9.10
14	$13.47	$13.50	$13.51
15	$15.57	$16.65	$14.38
16	$17.84	$15.79	$19.62
17	$30.66	$27.65	$35.61
18	$40.10	$70.57	$24.86

TIME FOR KIDS

Earth's Magnetic Field

Man of Steel

Richard Serra turns molten lead into works of art.

Magnetic Earth

Earth's magnetic field keeps humans and animals from getting lost.

The Earth is surrounded by a magnetic field. Why? Scientists don't know for sure, but most think it starts deep inside Earth, in its core. There, hot, liquid iron is constantly moving because of forces inside the core combined with Earth's rotation. Scientists believe this movement of hot metal is what gives Earth its magnetic field. It is as if there is a giant bar magnet inside Earth.

On the surface of the Earth, the magnetic field is not very strong, but it is very important. It is what makes compasses work. Inside each compass is a magnetized needle. One end of the needle is pointed or painted red. This is the "north-seeking" end. The needle sits on a loose base, so it can turn easily. The north-seeking end is attracted to one end of Earth's magnetic field—the end that points north. So the compass points north, too. Knowing this made it possible for early explorers to find their way, travel to new lands, and make maps.

Roger Harris/Photo Researchers, Inc.

▲ The curved lines show Earth's magnetic field.

Harald Sund/Getty Images

Image Source

▲ The needle on a compass points north.

▲ Migrating birds use Earth's magnetic field to find their way.

When North Becomes South

If you could travel back in time 80 million years, and if you had a compass with you, you would probably get lost pretty quickly. Unlike today, the north-seeking needle on your compass would point south. That's because at that time—and many times before and since—Earth's magnetic field was reversed. It turns out that Earth's magnetic field can and does change.

Every so often—every 250,000 years, on average—Earth's magnetic field reverses completely. It has happened many, many times in Earth's history, and is likely to happen again. The reversal doesn't happen suddenly. It's a process than can take hundreds of thousands of years. Even so, big changes in Earth's magnetic field could make it tougher for humans and animals to find their way home. — *Lisa Jo Rudy*

Solar Interference

Heat and light from the sun make life possible on Earth. But the sun can sometimes cause problems for us too.

Our nearest star is a fiery ball of gas with a stormy surface that burns at 11,000 degrees Fahrenheit. Solar flares are bursts of energy that shoot far into space from the sun's surface. Sunspots are cooler patches on the surface that form where the sun's magnetic field is very strong.

Every 11 years the number of solar flares and sunspots increases. These bursts of energy can affect Earth's magnetic field and disrupt our communications systems. If we have astronauts in orbit, they can be harmed by the radiation.

SOHO-EIT Consortium/ESA/NASA

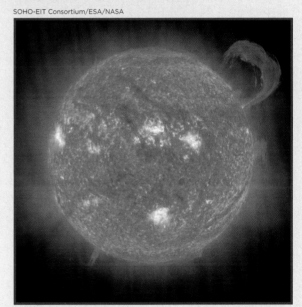

Solar flares and sunspots can both cause problems on Earth.

Sunspots from 1993–2004

Year	1993	1994	1995	1996	1997	1998	1999	2000	2001	2002	2003	2004
Sunspots	657	359	210	103	258	769	1,118	1,143	1,331	1,245	763	486
Solar flares	2,541	1,066	639	280	790	2,423	3,963	4,474	3,597	3,223	1,552	728

Source: National Aeronautics and Space Administration and the National Oceanic and Atmospheric Administration

Richard Serra: *Artist*

Some people use steel to erect buildings or make machines. Others use steel to make art.

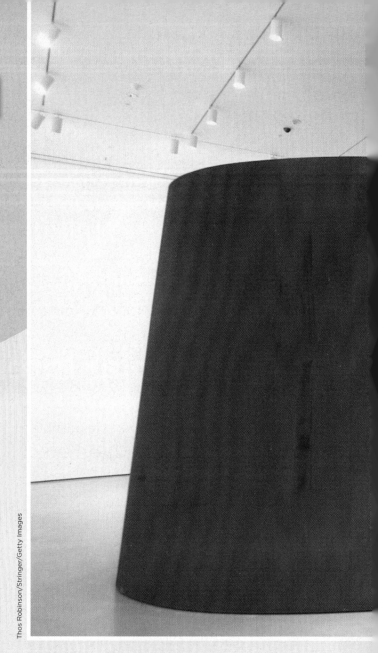

Thos Robinson/Stringer/Getty Images

Richard Serra used to fling ladles full of hot lead at the wall. He won awards for doing it. Serra is an artist. Lead is just one of the materials he uses to express his ideas.

As a young man, Serra made his sculptures out of fiberglass and rubber. But he worked in a steel mill to make money to help pay for college. At the steel mill, he got to know a lot about metal. When he graduated, he started to work with lead, iron, and steel.

When Serra started throwing molten lead against the wall in the name of art, people took notice. Later, he decided that it would be interesting to work with huge metal objects and gravity. He created gigantic lead plates and pipes called "prop pieces." They got their name from the fact that he propped them up against one another without using anything else to hold them up. One of the best known of these pieces was called "One Ton Prop (House of Cards)." The piece was just four squares of lead leaning against one another to form a cube. With nothing else holding it up, the cube really was like a delicately balanced house of cards. It didn't fall, but if it had, it would have made a tremendous crash!

Serra creates his sculptures by bending steel at very high temperatures.

As Serra became more famous, he was paid to create sculptures for outdoor parks. He used big steel plates to build a series of sculptures called "Torqued Ellipse." These sculptures are made up of steel plates, 13 feet high, formed into twisted ovals with a gap on one side to allow viewers to enter.

Richard Serra and one of his works of art ▶

The twisted ovals were so popular that Serra was asked to create even more outdoor sculptures. He created huge steel spirals and rippling bands of steel. He built spaces in which visitors could wander, exploring the texture and shape of space.

Though Serra does nothing to the surface of the steel, he bends it at high temperatures and leaves it out in the rain. As a result, the surfaces of his pieces are covered with stress patterns; splatter stains; and long, shallow ruts. Then, they rust. They look a little like a weathered cliff and a little like a painting.

Richard Serra was asked to put on a one-man show at New York City's Museum of Modern Art. First, though, museum staff had to make sure the floors wouldn't fall in. After all, just one of Serra's pieces weighs 243 tons. (An average airplane weighs just 199 tons!) — *Lisa Jo Rudy*

Jose Simal/EPA/Corbis

▲ A museum visitor explores Serra's work from the inside.

Sculpture Gardens

We are all familiar with museums—buildings that display works of art and other valuable objects— but have you ever heard of a sculpture garden? A sculpture garden is an outdoor space committed to the presentation of sculptures. Unlike indoor museums, sculpture gardens offer large, open areas that can accommodate massive sculptures. Sculpture gardens are located all over the country. In fact, many popular museums have them. The next time you visit a museum see if they have a sculpture garden. You may discover some amazing works of art.

Constantin Moisei/Alamy

▲ **Claes Oldenburg and Coosje van Bruggen's "Spoonbridge and Cherry" is on display at the Minneapolis Sculpture Garden in Minneapolis, MN.**

Metal Might

Metals make up more than 75 percent of the elements in the periodic table. A metal is an element that conducts heat and electricity well. Metals are usually solid at room temperature and are shiny when polished. They can be bent or flattened into shape without breaking. Examples of metals include aluminum, copper, gold, and silver. Some metals, such as iron, are magnetic. Can you find a metal on the periodic table?

Periodic Table of Elements

KEY

4 → Atomic Number
Be → Element Symbol

Metals
Metalloids
Nonmetals

1	2											13	14	15	16	17	18
1 H																	2 He
3 Li	4 Be											5 B	6 C	7 N	8 O	9 F	10 Ne
11 Na	12 Mg	3	4	5	6	7	8	9	10	11	12	13 Al	14 Si	15 P	16 S	17 Cl	18 Ar
19 K	20 Ca	21 Sc	22 Ti	23 V	24 Cr	25 Mn	26 Fe	27 Co	28 Ni	29 Cu	30 Zn	31 Ga	32 Ge	33 As	34 Se	35 Br	36 Kr
37 Rb	38 Sr	39 Y	40 Zr	41 Nb	42 Mo	43 Tc	44 Ru	45 Rh	46 Pd	47 Ag	48 Cd	49 In	50 Sn	51 Sb	52 Te	53 I	54 Xe
55 Cs	56 Ba	57 La	72 Hf	73 Ta	74 W	75 Re	76 Os	77 Ir	78 Pt	79 Au	80 Hg	81 Tl	82 Pb	83 Bi	84 Po	85 At	86 Rn
87 Fr	88 Ra	89 Ac	104 Rf	105 Db	106 Sg	107 Bh	108 Hs	109 Mt	110 Ds	111 Rg	112 Uub	113 Uut	114 Uuq	115 Uup	116 Uuh	117 Uus	118 Uuo

57 La	58 Ce	59 Pr	60 Nd	61 Pm	62 Sm	63 Eu	64 Gd	65 Tb	66 Dy	67 Ho	68 Er	69 Tm	70 Yb	71 Lu
89 Ac	90 Th	91 Pa	92 U	93 Np	94 Pu	95 Am	96 Cm	97 Bk	98 Cf	99 Es	100 Fm	101 Md	102 No	103 Lr

Honoring Art and Artists

Chuck Pefley/Alamy

The National Medal of Arts is the highest award given to artists by the United States Government. It is awarded by the President to individuals or groups for "outstanding contributions to the excellence, growth, support and availability of the arts in the United States." The awards are given in all categories of the arts. Between 1985 and 2007, nine sculptors received the award. Their backgrounds reflect the diversity of the people of the United States.

Year	Sculptor	Background
1987	Isamu Noguchi (1904-1988)	Japanese American; born in Los Angeles, CA, raised in Japan; moved to the U.S. in 1918
1989	Walker Kirtland Hancock (1901-1998)	Born in St. Louis, MO
1992	Allan Houser (1914-1994)	Native American, of the Chiricahua Apache tribe; born in Fort Sill, OK
1995	Roy Lichtenstein (1923-1997)	Born in New York, NY
1997	Louise Bourgeois (1911-)	Born in Paris, France; moved to the U.S. in 1938
1999	George Segal (1924-2000)	Born in New York, NY; parents were Jews who had emigrated from Eastern Europe
2000	Claes Oldenburg (1929-)	Born in Stockholm, Sweden; moved to the U.S. in 1936
2004	Frederick Hart (1943-1999)	Born in Atlanta, GA
2006	Viktor Schreckengost (1906-2008)	Born in Sebring, OH

Allan Houser's sculpture "As Long As the Waters Flow" is a tribute to Native Americans. It stands on the plaza of the Oklahoma State Capitol in Oklahoma City. ▶

Alan Copson/JAI/Corbis

TIME FOR KIDS

Dead Zones

GROWING PAINS!

The world's increasing population requires additional natural resources.

Are We Killing the Oceans?

Dead zones spread in the world's oceans.

A map of the Mississippi Gulf Coast region. ▼

The world's oceans are teeming with life, from microscopic organisms to whales, the largest animals on Earth. In a strange twist, however, we may be killing the oceans, or at least large parts of them. Human activity on land is creating "dead zones" in coastal waters around the globe.

Over the past four decades, these dead zones have appeared in almost 150 places, mostly in Europe and the east coast of the United States. Some are less than one square mile, and some are vast. The dead zone in the Gulf of Mexico is 7,000 square miles, or about the size of New Jersey.

Our oceans overflow with animal and plant life. Unlike the rest of the ocean, no animals live in dead zones. The reason is that the water below the surface has no oxygen in it. Without oxygen, fish or other animals cannot survive.

Too Much of a Good Thing

The causes of ocean dead zones are as clear as day. They can be traced to places far away from the coastline.

Chemical fertilizer used on farms and lawns is the main cause. Pollution from power plants and other industries adds to the problem. Runoff caused by rain and soil erosion carries fertilizer and other chemicals into a river. Then, the river carries them along toward the ocean. The river flows into the ocean, and all those chemicals are dumped in one place. That's why ocean dead zones usually appear at the mouths of rivers. Giant river systems, like the Mississippi, collect runoff fertilizer from millions of square miles.

This photo taken by a NASA satellite shows the Mississippi River carrying tons of sediment into the Gulf of Mexico.

Oxygen-starved zones created by fertilizer runoff are spreading.

Pilar Olivares/Reuters/Corbis

Algae blooms like this are a major reason why ocean dead zones form. ▼

Nati Harnik/Wide World Photos/AP Images

On land fertilizer helps plants grow. When fertilizer reaches the oceans, it feeds tiny plants called algae. Just as on land, the abundance of food causes algae blooms. The surface of the ocean can be covered with algae for hundreds of miles. When the algae die, they sink to the bottom and are eaten by bacteria. The bacteria use oxygen and release carbon dioxide. As more and more algae die, more and more bacteria grow. Eventually the bacteria use up all the oxygen in the lower levels of the dead zone. Once all the oxygen is gone, nothing can live there. Like a broken scale, the ecosystem tips too far in one direction. There is no life at the bottom of the dead zones because there is too much life at the top.

Saving the Oceans

Governments around the world have been trying to come up with ways to halt the spread of these oxygen-free areas.

For example, in Europe governments along the Rhine River, a larger river like the Mississippi, have agreed to cut nitrogen levels in half. One solution is to plant trees and grasslands alongside rivers, especially at their mouths. These plants will soak up the fertilizer before it reaches the ocean. Reducing pollution from industry, the use of chemical fertilizer, and untreated sewage would go a very long way to solving the problem.

The solutions are clear, but few of them have been attempted on a large scale. As a result, the dead zones continue to grow. Much more work is needed if we are to make these stricken ocean zones well again. Most people agree it's a good cause.

Our Packed Planet

Six and a half billion people are putting a squeeze on Earth's resources.

A family in the United States

Chances are you just blinked your eyes. In that time three people were added to the world's population. Three may not seem like a lot, but three new people every second means the world's population is growing like weeds. It adds up to about 184 people every minute, 11,040 every hour, 264,960 every day, and 97 million every year! In the United States, the population isn't increasing quite as fast. The Census Bureau says that in the United States, there is a birth every 8 seconds, a death every 13 seconds, and a new immigrant arriving every 27 seconds. That equals one new American every 15 seconds.

In 1999 the official number of people on the planet reached 6 billion. It is very difficult to picture a number that large. If you made a stack of 6 billion pennies, it would be about 5,740 miles high!

Of course, population growth didn't stop in 1999. By 2007 another half a billion people had been added to the world.

A street scene in Dhaka, Bangladesh, where the population is growing fast. ▼

Population Pressure

Earth's population hasn't always expanded so quickly. In prehistoric times or in early civilizations, the population grew slowly. That's because people didn't live as long as they do today. Around the year 1 B.C., historians estimate the world population was about 300 million.

As time passed, better medical care and nutrition and cleaner water helped people live longer. Then population growth began to pick up speed. Still, the human population didn't reach 1 billion until around 1800. It hit 3 billion around 1950. It took just under fifty years for it to double to 6 billion. The U.S. Census Bureau estimates that at the current rate of increase, the population will hit 9 billion in the year 2050.

Today most of the growth is taking place in developing countries. Those are nations that are poor and don't have much industry. Unlike other nations, China took a drastic step to slow population growth. In 1979, it said that most parents could not have more than one child. Imagine a land where most kids have no brothers or sisters!

Growing Pains

Every new person added to the planet needs food, water, shelter, clothes, and fuel. More people means more cars, roads, schools, hospitals, and stores.

Homer Sykes/Alamy

In heavily populated China, the government can fine parents for having more than one child.

Those things require additional natural resources, including land and water.

Earth is a bountiful planet, but its riches are limited. Less than 1 percent of Earth's water can be used for drinking and washing. One out of every 13 people around the world does not always have enough clean water. Water shortages have hit many parts of the world. They also have taken their toll in the western United States. So has an increase in the population of this area's cities, including Las Vegas and Los Angeles. Too many people are using too much water, especially in the already dry areas of the southwestern United States.

Food shortages are even more common. Worldwide, one out of every seven people does not get enough to eat. Huge demands for food force farmers to overuse their land. Over time, the soil loses its nutrients and the farmland becomes useless for growing food.

As the world becomes more crowded, more land is needed to make way for growing cities and suburbs. Forests are cleared away. That's a problem because trees help soak up a gas called carbon dioxide. Humans produce carbon dioxide by burning certain fuels, including coal and oil. Fewer trees means more carbon dioxide in the atmosphere. The buildup of carbon dioxide traps heat and pollution above Earth.

Population growth is an issue of concern in the United States, too. It is the fastest growing country among industrialized nations. The population hit 300 million in 2006. That was a 50 percent increase in just 39 years. People in the United States have bigger cars and houses than they had in the past. There is also a demand for more cars and houses. On top of that, people tend to drive more. All of these factors put pressure on natural resources. The United States Forest Service reported in 2006 that the country loses 6,000 acres of open space each day.

Although every person uses the planet's resources, some people use a lot more than others. The richest billion people—especially Americans—use the most resources. They also produce the most waste.

A family in India

Will Kids Turn the Tide?

Of course, having 6.5 billion people also means that there is a blanket of brainpower covering the Earth. This intelligence can help figure out better ways to use our resources. The trick will be getting people to realize that we can't go on burning through the planet's treasures forever.

Bill Ryan of the United Nations Population Fund says wealthy countries like the United States have a responsibility to take better care of the planet and its growing population. He says today's kids have the greatest opportunity to help. "There are more young people alive now than at any other time in history. The decisions they make will change the world," Ryan says.

Top 5

Countries with the Largest Populations (2007)

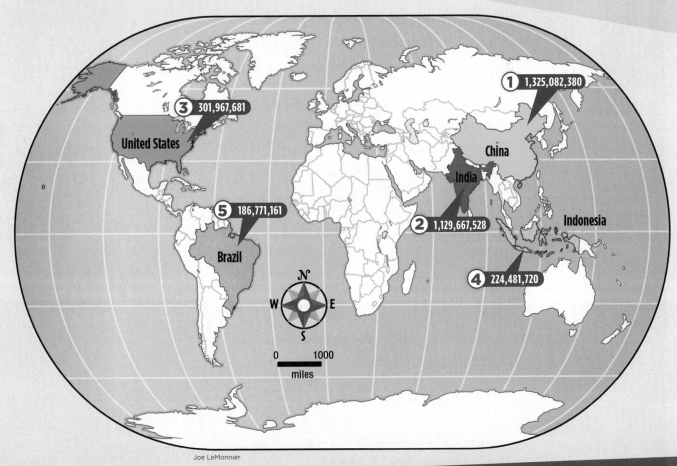

Joe LeMonnier

THE TYGER

By William Blake

Tyger! Tyger! burning bright
In the forests of the night,
What immortal hand or eye
Could frame thy fearful symmetry?

In what distant deeps or skies
Burnt the fire of thine eyes?
On what wings dare he aspire?
What the hand dare seize the fire?

And what shoulder, and what art,
Could twist the sinews of thy heart?
And when thy heart began to beat,
What dread hand? and what dread feet?

What the hammer? what the chain?
In what furnace was thy brain?
What the anvil? what dread grasp
Dare its deadly terrors clasp?

When the stars threw down their spears,
And water'd heaven with their tears,
Did he smile his work to see?
Did he who made the Lamb make thee?

Tyger! Tyger! burning bright
In the forests of the night,
What immortal hand or eye
Dare frame thy fearful symmetry?

TIME

FOR KIDS

Design
for Living

**Quilt patterns may have directed
enslaved people to freedom.**

The Amazing Watson

TFK talks with the scientist who helped unravel DNA.

▲ TFK reporter Noah Sneider interviews James Watson.

On February 28, 1953, James Watson of the United States and Francis Crick of England made a major scientific discovery that changed history. Then in 1962 they received the Nobel Prize, one of the world's highest honors.

According to Watson, Crick had announced, "We have found the secret of life."

What had these two scientists found that was so amazing? They had found the structure of DNA, the chemical that carries the recipe for every living thing. DNA is what makes an acorn grow into an oak tree instead of a palm tree. It is what makes a zebra have stripes. You, too, were born with your own DNA recipe.

TFK Kid Reporter Noah Sneider talked to Watson. Here are his questions (**Q**) and Watson's answers (**A**).

Q Fifty years ago you and Francis Crick solved the structure of DNA before anyone else did. What special talents or qualities allowed you to do that?

THE CODE OF LIFE

The recipe for making a human, a tulip, or a flea is carried in a chemical called DNA. It is shaped like a twisted ladder, or double helix. The rungs are made of four chemicals, abbreviated as A, C, G, and T. They are arranged in a unique pattern in every kind of living thing.

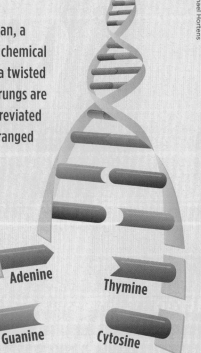

Adenine

Thymine

Guanine

Cytosine

A We were probably more interested in DNA than anyone else. It was the only scientific problem I wanted to think about.

Q Has progress in DNA study been faster or slower than you expected?

A Much faster. I didn't expect we would map the complete sequence of human DNA. This is three billion letters long!

Q What advances in DNA do you think will help the world most?

A My own particular ambition is to understand the genetic changes that give rise to cancer and to see this information used to treat cancer.

Q What advice would you give to kids who are interested in being scientists and making a discovery that could change the world?

A Read a great deal. You don't get anywhere by merely being bright. You have to know facts. Go to the best school you can get to and take courses by the best teachers. My advice is, have friends who are bright and don't have them because they're popular. Have friends who you can learn from.

GREAT IDEAS IN SCIENCE

Learning the shape of DNA has changed our world. Here are a few other important discoveries and inventions in science over the past hundred years.

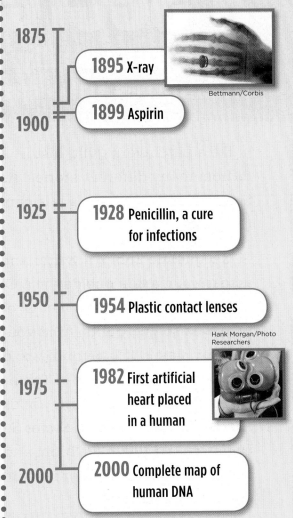

1875

1895 X-ray

Bettmann/Corbis

1900

1899 Aspirin

1925

1928 Penicillin, a cure for infections

1950

1954 Plastic contact lenses

Hank Morgan/Photo Researchers

1975

1982 First artificial heart placed in a human

2000

2000 Complete map of human DNA

◄ In 1953, Watson (left) and Crick posed with a DNA model in their lab in England.

A. Barrington Brown/ Photo Researchers

Unraveling a Secret Code

Did slaves really stitch messages into quilts?

Like a patchwork quilt, history is pieced together from many different stories, not all of them written. Sometimes one person's tale can change our view of the past.

Jacqueline Tobin, a writer and college professor, came across such a tale one day in a Charleston, South Carolina, marketplace. There she met Ozella McDaniel Williams, who was selling quilts. "Did you know that quilts were used by slaves to communicate on the Underground Railroad?" Williams asked Tobin. Her question sent Tobin on a five-year journey of discovery. In a book called *Hidden in Plain View: A Secret Story of Quilts and the Underground Railroad*, Tobin and coauthor Raymond Dobard stitched together research about slave quilts with one family's history.

Williams told an amazing narrative that had been handed down from her grandmother to her mother to her. She said the colors, patterns, and stitches of quilts formed a clandestine code used by slaves to guide them safely along the Underground Railroad, a system of escape routes to freedom for as many as 60,000 enslaved people.

According to Williams, each quilt pattern had a specific meaning. Slaves used quilt patterns both as "visual maps" to help remember important directions and warnings, and to send secret messages.

Myth or Fact?

David Blight, a professor at Yale University, and Giles Wright, an Underground Railroad expert with the New Jersey Historical Commission, are among the historians who question whether there really was a secret quilt code. When critics argue that it is only one family's story, Dobard responds, "Other families' stories are remarkably similar." Other historians point out that the quilt patterns discussed in the book did not exist in the 1800s or were too detailed for slaves to have had the time or the fabrics to create them.

When Oregon students asked Tobin about the quilt code, she admitted that some photographs in the book showed modern quilts made after the Civil War, but she also said that readers had misinterpreted the story. The quilts were not signals. Rather, the pattern names were used as mnemonic devices or ways to remember the route.

How would you solve this historical mystery?

Some people think the special patterns stitched into quilts like this one could have been used as directions to help escaped slaves find their way north. ▼

Patches That May Have Pointed the Way

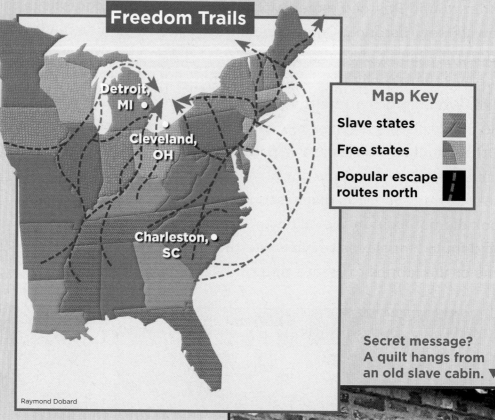

Freedom Trails

Detroit, MI

Cleveland, OH

Charleston, SC

Raymond Dobard

Map Key

Slave states

Free states

Popular escape routes north

Secret message? A quilt hangs from an old slave cabin. ▼

North Star
This popular quilt design is also known as the Star or the Evening Star. It might have told escaping enslaved people to follow the North Star.

Flying Geese
Because geese fly north in the spring, this pattern could have given two important instructions about when and how to travel.

Drunkard's Path
This pattern held a helpful warning, telling enslaved people to move in a zigzag pattern in order to avoid leaving a clear path for slave catchers to follow.

Raymond Dobard

Creative Codes

A code is a system of communication in which words, letters, or symbols are assigned meaning. Codes are often used for secrecy. During World War Two the Navajo code talkers played an important role in the United States Marine Corps. From 1942 to 1945 the code talkers transmitted secret messages by radio, telegraph, and telephone in their native language. These messages contained important information on troop movements and military strategy in the Pacific Ocean. The Japanese were never able to crack this creative code—which helped the United States win the battle of Iwo Jima.

Bettmann/Corbis

▲ Navajo code talkers serving in the U.S. Marines sent important military messages in secret code during World War Two.

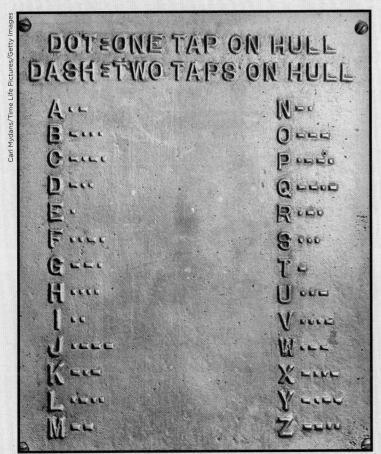

Carl Mydans/Time Life Pictures/Getty Images

◀ One of the most well known codes is Morse code. Created in the 1840s by Samuel F.B. Morse, it is used to send telegraph and radio messages. Sometimes it is used with flashes of light. Morse code uses patterns of dots and dashes to stand for each letter of the alphabet. Beats, marks, or pluses represent the dots and dashes. If you understand the code you can translate the patterns into words.

Harriet Tubman's Key Dates

The most famous "conductor" on the Underground Railroad was Harriet Tubman. Herself an escaped slave, she risked her life time and again to lead enslaved people to their freedom. Here are the highlights of her life.

Library of Congress

▲ Harriet Tubman escaped from slavery at age 29. Later she led about 300 slaves to freedom.

1820 Born in Bucktown, Maryland

1820

1840

1844 Marries John Tubman

1849 Uses the Underground Railroad to escape from slavery

1850 Makes the first of 19 trips to the South to free enslaved people

1860

1861 Begins four years of work for the Union army

1880

1897 Receives honor from England's Queen Victoria for bravery

1896 Buys land in Auburn, New York to build the Tubman Home

1900

H.B. Lindsley/Library of Congress

1913 Dies in Auburn, New York

1920

◄ Harriet Tubman lived until age 93.